NO
DYING
RACE

NO DYING RACE

CHARLES DUGUID

seal books
RIGBY

National Library of Australia
Cataloguing-in-Publication entry

Duguid, Charles, 1884–.
　No dying race.
　(Seal books).
　First published, Adelaide: Rigby, 1963.
　ISBN 0 7270 0664 9.
　[1.] Aborigines, Australian—History. I.
　Title. (Series).

994′.004′991

RIGBY LIMITED • ADELAIDE • SYDNEY
MELBOURNE • BRISBANE • PERTH
First published 1963
Published in Seal Books 1978

TO MY WIFE

*Always at one with me in my efforts
for recognition of the aborigines,
she many years ago gave me these
words of Ruskin*

I saw an injustice done and tried to remedy it. I heard falsehood taught and was compelled to deny it. Nothing else was possible to me. I knew not how little or how much might come of the business, or whether I was fit for it; but here was the lie, full set in front of me, and there was no way round it but only over it.

Acknowledgements

I wish to express my gratitude to Mr R. C. Seager of Victoria and to Mr Frank Halls of Waverley, Victoria, for photographs sent me for use in this book. Acknowledgement is also made to *The Advertiser* and *The News,* of Adelaide, each of which papers supplied a photograph. I thank, too, the Department of Territories and the Aboriginal Affairs Departments of the several States for information supplied me on request.

My greatest indebtedness is to my wife — wise critic and unfailing help.

Preface

Most Australians have little knowledge of our aborigines, and show little interest in their future. The aborigines are to become one with us, and it is with the hope of furthering that end that this book has been written. The earlier chapters relate some of the dealings, official and unofficial, of white Australians with dark Australians since 1928. They tell of my own travels in the Interior and in the Far North, of my continuing respect for our aborigines, and of my ever-deepening concern for their just and humane treatment.

The later portion of the book seeks to illustrate that the aborigines are people of equal worth with other Australians. It sets out the steps I consider necessary to bring them into equal enjoyment of Australian life.

Contents

Contents

Illustrations

PART I

1

Who Are They?

THE PRESENT ABORIGINES of the mainland of Australia—thought by some to be the third race to inhabit the continent—are akin to the Caucasian race, not to the Negroid or the Mongolian type. The discovery by R. T. Simmons and Dr J. J. Graydon at the Commonwealth Serum Laboratories, Melbourne, of "rare blood genes in Australian aborigines, the aboriginal Chenchus of southern India, and the white race suggests that there is an inherited blood component common to all three. They could all have sprouted from the same branch of the racial tree." An outstanding geneticist, Professor R. R. Gates, also classifies the aborigines as Caucasian.

It is significant that it was in the southern part of India that the aborigines of Australia were first specialized as a race, and from there migrated eastward and southward. They are thought to have reached Australia at the end of the last Ice Age, somewhere about ten thousand years ago, travelling by land except, perhaps, when they arrived at the very deep water that separates Borneo from Celebes, and Bali from Lombok. Alfred Russell Wallace has shown, in his *Island Life,* that the fauna and flora west of this line differ markedly from the biological life east of it. Deep water in these straits was evidently a dividing line, and the aborigines and their dingoes almost certainly crossed on rafts or canoes. It is interesting to note that, in the highlands of southern India, in Ceylon, in Malaya, and in the islands north of Australia which were then part of the land mass on which the aborigines travelled, people of similar type still exist.

Soon after the primitive aborigines reached this area it is believed the ocean level rose and cut them off from the rest of the world. Australia was then a most inhospitable land. There was no plant that could be coaxed into a fruit tree or a vegetable as we know them; there was no animal capable of giving milk for human use; there was no beast of burden. The white man

17

when he arrived failed, in spite of his knowledge, to improve on the native fauna and flora. Milk cows, beasts of burden, and all fruit trees and vegetable plants have been brought in from the outer world. The original Australians have in fact shown more intelligence, or perhaps one should say less greed, than the white immigrants; for the latter have in many parts of Australia grossly overstocked their pastures and damaged the land. In contrast the aboriginal groups, who knew intimately the tribal land allotted to them, moved over the area in a precise rotation and never ate out either game or vegetable food. In spite of the poorness of Australia as they found it, these nomads from India maintained a balance with nature until we came.

Their number then was at least 300,000 divided into some five hundred major groupings, each with its own tongue, and they covered the whole continent. By day the men, with spears and woomeras (spear-throwers), hunted the larger animals—kangaroos, euros, wallabies, and emus—while the women gathered vegetable food and the smaller animals. In the evening a low windscreen of brushwood was thrown up by the men, and at night individual members of the family slept between little fires with supplies of dry tinder ready to be pulled on to the embers as required.

Tribal organization covered the whole of their life. Their moral code and social etiquette were strictly observed; marriage laws were carefully evolved to prevent inbreeding; religion was part of their very being. In the material things of life full-blood aborigines are primitive, but they are of normal intelligence, and the struggle to keep alive has made them keenly observant and very inventive. When treated with understanding they are a co-operative and adaptable people. In characteristics they are much akin to us; they have a very strong love of family, and a keen sense of family obligation. Their aesthetic appreciation is highly developed, and is notable in acting, dancing, singing, and in their own decorative art. Their sense of humour appears to be as keen as our own.

The lack of any concerted and sustained attempt by the white race at any time to understand and to co-operate with the native people has been a costly mistake for both dark and white Australians.

The incomers were not interested in native skills and customs. They considered themselves superior to the aborigines in every

18

way, and if the natives did not like the way things were evolving —deprivation of their food supplies, the wrecking of their social organization, and an utter contempt for their spiritual heritage —then they must accept what was coming to them without demur. On that basis difficulties and misunderstandings were inevitable, and when white settlers moved inward from the coast away from constituted authority, the direction from the British Government—that the aborigines were to be accorded the same privileges and treatment as the Crown's other subjects —was forgotten.

In early pioneering days the native people were regarded at times almost as vermin and often deliberately destroyed as such. No State in Australia can deny a dark history of murder. In the late nineteenth century and also in the twentieth century the common attitude was that the race, although admittedly human, was incapable of development and was fast dying out.

With the marked increase in full-bloods in recent years, however, a new policy has come to light—that of assimilation. But officially it is stressed that in the process, the aborigines must wean themselves from their age-old culture and contacts. It is a serious criticism of our intelligence and character that, so late in the day, the old mistake of ignoring the contribution of our fine full-bloods is being repeated.

Not until 1914 did I actually see any aborigines. They were living among sand-dunes on the coast of South Australia in a galvanized iron shed that was neither windproof nor waterproof. One of them was suffering from pulmonary tuberculosis, and very ill. I reported their plight to the proper authorities, but was told that aborigines would not stay in houses. Nothing was done.

During the war and its aftermath I had forgotten about the aborigines, but in 1928 I was suddenly aroused. A wholesale shooting of weak, drought-stricken aborigines had taken place in the Northern Territory following the death of a white man —a dingo trapper. No attempt was made to find who was responsible, but eventually two aborigines were taken to Darwin, tried, and found not guilty. The policeman responsible for the shooting was not tried as were these two men. Only a police inquiry was held, and despite contradictory evidence by the policeman in question, the killings were adjudged justifiable

19

and he continued to serve in the police force as a Protector of Aborigines!

This case caused considerable disquiet in the settled southern part of Australia. It was, however, significant of the attitude of the Northern Territory to the aborigines thirty years ago that, at the very time when this massacre took place, the Queensland Chief Protector, the late J. H. Bleakley, was actually in the Territory as a Royal Commissioner inquiring into the treatment of aborigines there.

The prolonged and severe drought conditions in Central Australia at that time brought an appeal for rations for the starving aborigines from an itinerant missioner named E. E. Kramer. From Alice Springs to the South Australian border natural vegetable food was no longer available, native game had disappeared, and the rabbits had died off. There had been heavy losses in cattle, and no work was available for aboriginal stockmen on the cattle stations. The Aborigines Friends Association, for whom Mr Kramer worked among the natives, was informed by the Minister that the Government Resident, the Chief Protector of Aborigines, and the Sergeant of Police in Central Australia had conferred and were unanimous that to give effect to Mr Kramer's suggestion "would be wrong in principle." "Rations should be restricted to the aged and infirm only." Kramer was angry and ashamed at the Government's attitude; the people, he said, were subsisting on "husks, wind and water."

Soon after this a missionary from an island off Arnhem Land came to my consulting rooms in Adelaide. She had contracted leprosy from an aboriginal boy. At her weekly visits to my surgery she told me of the treatment of aborigines by men of our race in the far north—happenings which at that time seemed to me incredible. However, inquiries and investigations made by me in the years that followed have proved that my patient was right.

In contrast to this was the attitude of aborigines to white men in distress. In 1932 two German airmen in a flight from Timor were lost from 15 May to 22 June. Their aeroplane had presumably crashed in unknown country on the northern coast. They were in desperate straits and hardly able to swallow, when the aborigines from the Drysdale River Mission found them. The airmen were given water, and food was pushed into their mouths. One of the aborigines set off to the Mission to report the find, and guided a party back to the spot. The *West Australian* 14 June, 1932 reported that during the search by police and others, Sergeant— "conveyed his personal opinion to the Commissioner of Police that the aviators had either perished or had been murdered by blacks." When news of the rescue reached the police a constable went to the spot and reported "he was releasing all the natives whom he was holding as possible witnesses of the reported murder." Exactly ten years later a party of Dutch people were stranded on the north-west corner of Western Australia and would have perished had not a full-blood tribal aboriginal happened on them when hunting. He shared with them the food and water he was carrying, and later led them to a waterhole. He then walked forty miles for help.

My growing concern about a state of affairs to which most Australians seemed blind led me to make an appeal to my own Church. In September, 1933, at the General Assembly of the Presbyterian Church of Australia meeting in Melbourne, I spoke on aborigines and appealed for a nation-wide effort by Christians to put an end to the appalling injustices the aborigines were suffering. There was strong support from the great majority of the Assembly, but a few did not regard the treatment of aborigines as a vital issue.

In the previous month the nation had learnt of the killing of five Japanese trepang gatherers at Caledon Bay, Arnhem Land, in 1932, and of a constable at Woodah Island in Blue Mud Bay in 1933. From certain quarters came a demand for a punitive expedition, but a public outcry against this suggestion was raised, and the Government forbade an armed attack. In the end it was left to a missionary of the Church Missionary Society to induce the wanted tribal aborigines to travel by boat to Darwin. On arrival there the five men were locked up in police cells where, stated the *Advertiser* 12 April, 1934, "they showed the utmost terror, howling and wailing and shaking the bars of their cells like newly caged animals."

Next day the most pitiful scenes took place in the gaol and in the court. These tribal nomads of the wilds were handcuffed in their cells, dragged and pushed into court, where they turned pathetically to the missionary who had brought them. Takiar, one of the tribal leaders, completely ignorant of the proceedings, was condemned to death, but the High Court of Australia quashed the conviction and ordered his immediate release. Takiar was then taken from the death cell to the aboriginal compound. Two days later it was announced that he had escaped. But Takiar never reached home, and how far he got from Darwin and what happened to him has never been cleared up. We do know, however, what happened when he left his home at Blue Mud Bay on the eastern shore of Arnhem Land. The Rev J. R. Dyer, who travelled to Darwin on the same boat as the natives, writes in his book *Unarmed Combat* —"That morning Takiar came aboard of his own accord—a very sad scene. His parents, children, wives and all his relations wept aloud as we pushed off in the dinghy, and Takiar was in tears the greater part of the day."

During that same year—1933—a white man was tried for the fatal shooting of a native in the Northern Territory. According to the Crown Law Officer the aboriginal, Tchu Gora, had refused to tell the white man where his wife was. The jury of white men at the Supreme Court, Darwin, found the accused not guilty. Some years later I met that same white man travelling the bush with an aboriginal full-blood woman. Most of the serious trouble with the natives has been caused by white men associating with aboriginal women. If an aggrieved husband objected he could be dealt with, and a plea of self-defence put to the white jury if a trial eventuated.

It was also in 1933 that the Warramunga tribe was compelled by the Federal Government to leave their home country when gold was found on the Tennant Creek Aboriginal Reserve. The subsequent history of this tribe is told in the chapter "Protective Policies."

By the middle of 1934 my missionary patient with leprosy strongly urged me to go north and see things for myself. So in July 1 took the train to Alice Springs *en route* for Darwin with introductions from the Federal Government to the medical authorities there. But at Alice Springs—the railhead—I was asked by the Commonwealth Medical Officer to perform a major operation, and the mail-motor for Darwin had to leave without me. My first experience at Alice Springs was startling. While I was buying goods in a store the woman who served me asked why I had planned to go to Darwin. "In connection with leprosy among aborigines," I replied.

"You don't want to worry about abos," she said; "the sooner they're dead the better." And in the next three weeks I was to find this was a common attitude in the Inland.

There was no leprosy in the heart of the Continent, but there was plenty for me to do. I made an inspection of the living conditions of aborigines at Alice Springs and was officially asked to make an investigation into the health of the aborigines at Hermannsburg Mission. I visited cattle stations of the Inland and saw the conditions of aborigines there.

The Bungalow Compound at Alice Springs was then the home of half-caste children gathered from far and near. At that time they were not allowed to attend the local school, but remained at the Compound in the care of a white married couple. At the age of sixteen the girls were generally sent to work in homes on cattle stations, and the percentage who returned pregnant was very high. Other half-caste girls were helping in homes of Alice Springs' residents, very often being accommodated at the end of a veranda separated off by hessian. Their lot was not a happy one; there was no privacy, and most of them worked for long hours for very little pay—in some cases for food and clothing only.

Beyond the township, full-blood old men and women lived in the most miserable "humpies" built of scrap iron, old bags, or hessian. One had to stoop down to enter these hovels. Embers burned in the centre of the earth floor. Sunshine was effectively shut out, but there was little protection against rain.

Hermannsburg natives I found heavily infected with tuberculosis. They were living in very old thick-walled mud huts each with one small aperture, which was usually stuffed with rags. After a two-day survey of the Mission area I recommended that all the mud huts be razed to the ground. The superintendent asked me to go round the huts again next day. I did so, and emphasized that every hut was a source of infection.

Two years later, finding the huts gone, I said, "Well, you took my advice after all." "Not I," Pastor Albrecht told me, "the natives heard what you said, and as soon as you left they began knocking down the walls." I knew before making the survey that unless the disease could be brought under control it was almost certain the Mission would be closed. Hermannsburg owes a debt of gratitude to those old men who demolished the huts.

My visits to the cattle stations made me depressed and ashamed beyond measure. As I approached one homestead on a cold, cheerless, rainy day, old men, women, and children came running down a hillside. They were all painfully thin and hungry, their clothes were mere rags. Later, over a cup of tea in the homestead, I asked why the aborigines we had seen did not get more food. "They get Government rations," was the reply. At that time official instructions were as follows:

The rations or weekly allowance to each person receiving relief, must not exceed: Flour 5 lb., sugar 1 lb., tea ¼ lb.

Only aged, infirm, and sick natives were eligible. And when I discussed the matter with a policeman he pointed out to me the words "must not exceed."

On that visit to Alice Springs I found only one man doing anything for aborigines—Pastor E. E. Kramer. And, with one solitary exception, even ministers of the Christian Church were not interested. The Inland Missions of the Presbyterian and the Methodist Churches did not include aborigines in their ministry, and the Presbyterian Inland Mission Hostels did not in any circumstances admit aborigines. I was informed frankly that the Australian Inland Mission had no concern with "niggers," and representatives of both these Inland Missions assured me that if they paid attention to aborigines their work on behalf of the white people on cattle stations would soon come to an end. The Methodist ministers were not unsympathetic towards the aborigines, but every padre of the Australian Inland Mission whom I met at that time regarded the natives as unworthy of attention, and they treated them accordingly—with contempt and scorn.

As a Presbyterian I was deeply ashamed, and puzzled why that Mission, founded in 1912, should claim that its founder was a lady in Scotland who set money aside in 1839 "for the education and evangelization of the Aborigines in South Australia." It seemed extraordinary in view of the mission's attitude to aborigines that it should make this claim. Not till 1958 were people of any aboriginal blood admitted to the hostels.

On this Alice Springs visit I met many people from the South who had come North in the hope that the dry climate would cure them of their lung trouble. It was not difficult to understand why tuberculosis had taken such a toll of the aborigines —they were virgin soil, and they were poorly fed.

There was no interest in, let alone any security for, up-country aborigines at that time. Full-bloods received no education whatever; and half-castes very little.

2

Wages And Conditions

WAGES OF full-bloods in 1934 were negligible. Federal ordinance decreed that for aborigines working on cattle stations wages were to be paid into a trust fund at the rate of five shillings a week, but if station managers agreed to feed dependants of the worker no payment need be given. And that was the general custom. Aborigines working in townships were to receive three shillings a week, and two shillings was entered in a trust fund. If they were employed on mining leases, by prospectors, or by hawkers they were paid at the rate of five shillings a week as a credit to their trust account. Before an aboriginal man left the township where he was engaged he might ask for a bag of flour for his wife and children—"lubras" and "picanninies" were the terms my informant used—or he might ask that they get supplies from time to time in his absence. But the Police Protector was not supposed to suggest this course of action. It was the native's actual request he needed, and not just his consent. If the women and children were not provided for in this way they were not eligible for rations.

Aborigines who went droving were paid at the rate of twenty-four shillings a week while travelling with stock, and sixteen shillings weekly while travelling with plant only. The white drover in charge provided food, but the wages were held in trust by the Police Protector at the man's home area pending his return. On this point extracts from a letter of David Cahill, grazier, to the *Northern Standard* 25 April, 1933 are revealing.

> These blacks [in gaol] were charged at Borroloola with cattle killing. Four of them were on the road with myself and my partner droving cattle for which they were paid at the ruling rate of wages. These wages were paid to the Police Sergeant at Borroloola on July 18th, 1932. These boys left here on 6th November, 1932 to try to

get their wages. All they got was 10/- for which they had to walk 69 miles in and the same distance back. They left here again on Nov. 27th to try to get some more of their wages from the Protector. On this occasion they got another 10/- each. I wonder how a salaried official would like to walk a distance of 138 miles for the sake of collecting 10/- he earned five or six months previously. These boys had enough money held by the Protector to help them until they were employed again, and now instead of getting their wages they are serving a long term of imprisonment for which I have a statement from several black witnesses for an alleged offence they were never guilty of.

Horace Foster, reporting in the same newspaper on 12 October, 1933 on the inquiry into Cahill's charges against police in connection with alleged cattle killing said:

Sergeant— stated that two witnesses had shown him the carcase that all the trouble was about, and that the carcase was there just as the cow died. Mr.—, manager of the Robinson River Station, also in court, swore that he left the cow very near dead, and that when he returned a long time afterwards, the whole bones and hide were there not touched. . . .

Cahill had made a further charge.

I met Constable— on the Foelsche on 28th June, 1933. He took a boy named Cliff out of my camp and charged him with spearing a beast six months previously. As the boy was in my employment at that time I offered to go as a witness on his behalf. Then P.C.— changed the killing to a later date. This conversation took place in the presence of another white person.

The lot of aborigines at that time was indeed hopeless. In June, 1934 in Shepparton, Victoria, Mr J. R. Wilkinson, of the Methodist Inland Mission service, made most serious allegations of brutal cruelty to aborigines by policemen in the Northern Territory, some of whom were named. He affirmed he had made an official complaint without result. The Department of the Interior denied the allegations whereupon Mr Wilkinson, according to the *Advertiser,* 19 June, 1934, said he was prepared at any time and before any tribunal to substantiate his assertions.

Examination of the law relating to aborigines in the Northern Territory in the early nineteen-thirties revealed the fact that in spite of a man's ludicrously poor wage, three shillings a week and two shillings in a trust fund with the police, no definite provision was made for his wife and children, no matter how he was employed, except in the case of employment on a cattle station exempt from paying wages. And there was no unemployment relief for workers. In times of drought the working natives were not needed on the cattle stations, yet they had to find food. Many of them had lost the art of tracking game, and of course animals do not stay long in drought-stricken country. Eventually a bullock might be speared, in which case the matter would be reported to the police, and anyone found in possession of bullock-beef was brought into Alice Springs for trial. If found guilty he would be sentenced to six to nine months in gaol with hard labour. This generally meant chopping a supply of firewood. There never seemed to be any difficulty in getting labour for that job.

Ashamed of the conditions I had found in the cattle country in 1934, I determined the following year to see how aborigines fared in their own tribal lands. And so, with two friends, I left Adelaide by car for the Musgrave Ranges, a thousand miles away in the far north-west corner of South Australia.

The northern agricultural area of the State was in very poor heart, and although it was almost mid-winter we left Quorn in a fierce dust-storm. Beyond Hawker we travelled on a wind-swept track, with large loose stones and deep ruts. The township of Farina was heavily banked up with sand—in fact it was almost hidden—and from there to Marree we had to cross three stretches of sand, at the last of which we were forced to roll out our coconut matting in order to get through. West of Marree several sandhills had to be negotiated, and at the steepest the matting had to be used again to enable the car to get over the top.

Sand was not the only trouble, for after a time we had to cross a stretch of country strewn with sharp-edged boulders, one of which cut right through a tyre. It was a relief to reach the edge of Lake Eyre and travel for a while on smooth ground.

In the two hundred and seventy miles between Marree and Oodnadatta there was only one hotel—at William Creek—where we sought directions to Anna Creek Cattle Station, the manager of which was Archie McLean, an old patient of mine. Ten more miles in the dark and we were thankful to see lanterns being waved vigorously on the far side of the creek, and to get a warning not to cross at that spot. After a hearty meal, reminiscences in front of a log fire, and eight hours dead to the world we were up early for another strenuous day.

After breakfast the manager and I inspected the native camp. This was clean and well kept; and there was respect between master and man. The aborigines were said to have suffered severely from colds in the winter, due to insufficient food and clothing. Rabbits were virtually extinct.

At midday with considerable misgiving we crossed the very stony Algebuckina Creek and stopped for lunch on the far bank.

At Oodnadatta, the State's most northerly town, we struck west and soon came face to face with the intermingling of white and dark Australians. There were three cattle stations in the next hundred miles, but west of these the country was being opened up in five hundred-acre blocks by men with little capital. Before the block was granted, an adequate supply of water had to be assured—by the sinking of wells.

Lying in our swags, one night in that area, we noted two widely separated camp fires in the bush. Morning revealed in each camp a white man and a native woman. Another morning as we were rousing from sleep we saw a white man, his native woman, and three children break camp. They had slept in the dry bed of a creek not far from us. Nearly all white men within a hundred miles of the Musgraves were living with native women.

Soon after leaving the last cattle station on the direct route westward we took a wrong turning. This added greatly to our mileage, but also to our knowledge. To get our bearings we pulled in at a lonely homestead, where the owner and his wife were very nervous at our approach. They told us afterwards they thought we might have been detectives. A rifle lay on the kitchen table, and a revolver on the mantlepiece; both firearms were kept loaded. I knew the aboriginal man who had been shot at this station the previous year. He was in hospital in Adelaide for sixteen weeks, waiting for his shattered thigh-bone to knit, and for his pulped head to heal.

Marla Bore was the next landmark, and soon afterwards a hut came in view. The occupants—a white man and a lubra—were not at home; they were on the Aborigines Reserve collecting dingo scalps from the tribal natives. We turned sharply to the right here, and over a rise saw Wantapella Swamp, a great expanse of water, which we had to skirt, and in doing so sent a herd of cattle into a gallop.

Another fifteen miles took us to the main track and soon after, as the light was failing, we camped for the night at Moorilyana, a great outcrop of huge granite rocks. The night was absolutely still, and after sleeping soundly under the stars we rose at daybreak. The route to the Musgraves was by Echo Hill, and in the late afternoon, a week after we had left Adelaide, we reached an unfinished house at the entrance to the Ranges. The man who lived there kept some sheep, but most of his income came from collecting dingo scalps from the tribal aborigines. The native received a small quantity of flour for these, and the "dogger" got seven shillings and sixpence for each scalp. The amount now paid by the Government is one pound.

My travelling companions got to work on the car—it had had a battering—tubes and tyres had to be repaired, a broken pin on the self-starter mended, and cylinder head and carburettor gaskets adjusted somehow. Under the guidance of a young part-aboriginal man with whom I have since kept in contact I spent my time exploring the near-by mountains.

One evening when hurrying home in the failing light I was suddenly and literally brought to a standstill by a spider's web stretched across the path. When I examined it I was amazed at the strength of this web.

The aborigines in the Ranges were naked nomads, as their forebears had been for thousands of years, and they had a dignity that was striking. While we were at this place two tribal girls arrived on foot with a letter for the owner of Ernabella from another small station-owner living sixty miles north in the Northern Territory. On the same day a young native woman leading a camel loaded with provisions set off for a white man's camp twenty miles further west in the Ranges. He too was a "dogger." Twelve years later a well-dressed aboriginal woman spoke to me in Adelaide. It was the camel driver I had met in the Ranges; she was happily married and living in the city—another example of the adaptability of the aboriginal race.

On the return trip from the Musgraves we met a constable and two settlers on their way to the Ranges to arrest tribal aborigines suspected of sheep killing. It was the old story—the white man took over more and more tribal country on which to fatten sheep or cattle. The aborigines, who had always lived by hunting game in that same country, might understandably spear a sheep and share it as they were tribally bound to do. It is not difficult to see the new settler's point of view: he reported the matter to the police, natives went to gaol, and disintegration of the tribe set in. It was accepted across Australia that the native even in his own land had no rights to it —in spite of the fact that by law he was supposed to maintain access to the water and game on his tribal land, now a cattle station.

While we were in this area a tragedy occurred at Ayers Rock, a hundred miles to the north. A native was shot dead by a policeman on patrol when he did not come out of a cave when called on to do so. A board of inquiry later visited the scene with the accused constable, who voluntarily acted as cook on the trip and did the camp chores. The finding given, in September, 1935, was "that the shooting of the aborigine, though legally justified, was not warranted."

In spite of this finding the policeman continued as a Protector of Aborigines and rose to one of the highest positions in the police force. On his retirement he gave a statement to the Press in which he said he had learnt never to be weak with natives.

He justified the chaining of aborigines by the neck, saying that they had freedom to move their limbs when on the move during the day, and when chained to trees at night they were free to move round the trees. He claimed he had defied a Government order in 1940 to stop chaining by the neck.

A few miles out from the Musgrave Ranges the repaired cylinder-head gasket failed, but we decided to continue on two cylinders and reached Lambina cattle station late at night. It had been an anxious all-day trip through creeks and over gibber stones, and we were ready for our swags; but Mr and Mrs Page insisted on our first having a hearty meal. Less than three years later the Lambina homestead was washed away in a devastating flood—the worst ever known in the district. When the waters subsided a truck and a buggy were found in the highest branches of near-by gum trees. The homestead and station buildings were a complete loss.

The trip from Lambina to Oodnadatta proved uneventful despite Mr Page's fears for us, with the damaged gasket and no spare tyre. However, a very significant incident happened at the township soon after our arrival. The policeman's wife— her husband was out on patrol—sought my help. She had received a message an hour or two before that an aboriginal was being brought from a distant cattle station to the police station; that he was dangerous, a raving lunatic, and would not eat. I had to go beyond the township for a time, but on my return I was asked to examine the man, who had been brought in on a buckboard.

A black tracker took me to a cell. It was very small, dark, and cold, both seat and floor being of stone slabs. The man had a heavy chain padlocked on his neck, and his wrists were handcuffed. He was very cold, and had an expressionless look on his sunken face. His clothing consisted of shirt, jacket, trousers, and khaki overcoat; no buttons anywhere, and no belt. The black tracker was loath to remove the handcuffs when told to do so, but I left him in no doubt as to my meaning.

I then removed the man's clothing, and wrote down my findings during the examination. The man was painfully thin, with depressions above and below the collar-bones. His wrists and hands were swollen with recent chafing on the back of the right hand and lower part of the right forearm. Both bones in the lower half of the right forearm were bent and fixed, the result of an old, untreated fracture. There were old scars on both forearms and upper arms, and two fairly recent ones on his chest. His shoulder blades and the left side of his back over the lower ribs also showed recent injury.

The man was ravenous when offered food, and on my instructions was fed for the first twenty-four hours little and often with warm bread and milk. The manner in which the policeman's wife catered for the native was very fine. When he was given full meals he simply gulped them down. In a month's time he was brought to Adelaide for treatment at the Mental Hospital,

Old man of Pitjantjatjara tribe, Musgrave Ranges.

Lesson in spear throwing. Pitjantjatjara tribe, Musgrave Ranges.

Grub-time at Ernabella.

and two months later he was hardly recognizable as the same man.

An interesting sequel to this incident occurred the following year. One evening in a country town I gave an illustrated lecture about this trip. At the end of my talk a young man came angrily forward to me. Stretching out his left hand for everyone to see he said, "That nigger you showed broke a bone in my hand with a hammer when I was breaking him in. What would you have done?" He was speechless with rage when I answered: "I wouldn't have hit you on the hand; you would have got it on the head!"

At Oodnadatta my two friends were busy making a thorough overhaul of the car and fitting replacements while I visited the native camp situated on the edge of the local rubbish dump. Here, in the most miserable hovels, made of old iron sheets and bags from the dump, aboriginal families were living. Men and women from the camp worked for townsfolk during the day for pitiful reward. I made several visits, too, to six half-caste children who were being cared for in a Home of the United Aborigines Mission. This was the only place in Oodnadatta where respect was shown to anyone of aboriginal blood.

The back-track to Adelaide had lonely, waterless stretches, and there was no hotel in the six hundred miles to Port Augusta; but the surface was good, and as the car was now running well and we were carrying ample supplies of water we decided to return that way. The road ran west for eighty miles before turning south at Hawk's Nest Well. In the next forty miles were two cattle stations—Wintinna, where we had a cup of tea, and Mt Willoughby, where we stayed the night.

Seventy-five miles further south we came on a cattle station in the first stage of development. The bedroom was a tent, the living room and kitchen a hessian enclosure with dirt floor, and the shed for wagon and horses was built of unfashioned tree trunks, and had a brushwood roof. Near by was a waterhole fast drying up, and one well. The husband was out mustering, but his wife very kindly gave us a cup of tea which we thoroughly enjoyed, especially as seven miles back we had been delayed in the heat with a badly punctured tyre.

Our next stop, twenty miles further on, was one of the most interesting and unusual places in the whole of Australia—the Coober Pedy opal fields. We called at the store for petrol, and

33

were given a meal with the usual outback hospitality. In those early days of 1935 the post office and store were actually dug-outs in the hillside, as were the homes of the more permanent gougers. About eighty miles south of Coober Pedy we came on the dog fence, the outer limit of the sheep country. Any sheep north of this fence must be shepherded. The dingo is greatly dreaded by sheep farmers, and one has to be sure that gates that have been opened are always left securely shut.

At the end of an hour's travelling inside the fence we saw a light. It came from The Twins Station, and we were invited to stay the night.

We got petrol ten miles further on at Mt Eba Station, a very up-to-date place. Because of the winding nature of the track it was slow travelling for the next seventy miles to East Well Station, where we were warmly welcomed by Mr and Mrs Jock Pick. In another twelve miles we joined the main road which, however, was actually much rougher than the bush track. Sixty miles on in the evening we pulled up alongside a disabled double-decker truck and were glad to be able to help the driver and his mate by carrying the damaged part to Port Augusta for repair.

As we drove on in the dark, kangaroos, dazzled by the headlights, kept jumping in front of the car, and one cleared the bonnet. Soon afterwards we camped for the night, immediately lit a fire, and threw up a bush breakwind to give us some shelter from a bitterly cold wind. The wind was so strong that we even made use of our car seats to reinforce the breakwind.

Next day at Port Augusta I inspected the aborigines' camp. The shacks were of better construction than those further north, but they were utterly unhygienic. Again, no one accepted responsibility for aborigines.

On my return to Adelaide I reported to the Minister responsible for aborigines in South Australia—the late Sir Herbert Hudd. I asked that the Government should take steps to save the last remaining intact tribe in the State, the people in the Musgrave Ranges. Mr Hudd, as he then was, asked for a statement in writing, which he placed before Cabinet. The area covered by me was then investigated by the Government.

Two months later the Minister asked if I would care to submit a scheme that would save the tribe I had encountered and help to eliminate the breeding and neglect of illegitimate half-caste children. My plan was then carefully considered by Cabinet.

Eventually I was informed that if I could get a responsible church to give continuity to the scheme and collect a thousand pounds, the Government would give a similar amount. I made it my business to collect that money.

The essential features of the plan were that in any mission or settlement established there should be respect for native customs, that all members of the mission staff should be persons trained in a particular sphere of work and should learn the native language thoroughly. Responsibility was to be passed to the natives as soon as they were willing and able to take it.

In the early years of school life the native language was to be used, and English later taught as a foreign language. There was to be no compulsion in education or religion. Attention to the health of the natives was to be a special feature. These provisions have been justified. There is no inferiority complex at Ernabella, the mission founded on these lines; pidgin English has never been spoken, and the fact that the white staff had to learn the language of the aborigines has established a tradition of co-operation between the two peoples.

On the 1935 trip to and from the Musgraves we had made friends with part-aboriginal children in the care of the United Aborigines Mission at Oodnadatta and Quorn. I had suggested to Sister Hyde at Quorn that they should all visit Adelaide, and in December of that year thirty-four children and mission staff came to my home and grounds for a six weeks' holiday in Adelaide. It was the first impact on Adelaide of a group of young aborigines from the north, and during their stay the children were introduced by various religious organizations, to the many aspects of city life.

This was the first of a number of such educational holidays, and today many of those youngsters of 1935 are in responsible positions in our community.

3

Haast Bluff

MY NEXT TRIP to the Inland was planned for the winter of 1936, and this time I had with me the Rev David Munro, who had succeeded me as Moderator of the Presbyterian Church in South Australia. I was anxious that he should see for himself the conditions that I had been agitating about for the previous two years. I felt confident that after this trip he would be deeply concerned, and as Moderator of the Church would lend his full support to the mission project already approved by the Government. The feeling of the Government on the matter can be judged by the following excerpt from the Report of the Chief Protector of Aborigines for the year ended 30 June, 1936:

> In the north west, that is the large aboriginal reserve and the country contiguous to it, the aboriginals in South Australia are making their last stand as a body of pure-blooded individuals not yet degraded by contact with a civilization they cannot assimilate, and understand, and it will be to the advantage of the aboriginal and the State to keep them as such for as long as possible. It appears to be impossible to stop the progress of the white race, even if it does upset the life and habits of the indigenous people. It therefore becomes our duty to buffer the contact in some way so that the clash will not only be gradual, but will in the first instance be with persons who have the welfare and love of the aborigines at heart, and not with those who wish to use him for their own personal gain, discarding him once he has served their purpose. Doctor Charles Duguid has been urging this duty upon the people of South Australia and is endeavouring to get support for a scheme, which, gaining by the errors of missionary enterprise in the past, will serve to assist the aboriginal to retain his virility and

36

self-respect and save him from the general degradation which usually follows his association with white settlement.

On 4 June we left Adelaide by train for Alice Springs *en route* for the tribal country westward of Haast Bluff. On arrival there we visited the native camp beyond the town, and the native "hospital," a galvanized iron shanty. My old friend Dow Dow, who was a boy at Alice Springs when the first white men arrived, was on a near-by hillside. While I was with him his grandson of about twenty-four with his young wife and baby arrived. The young man was in stockman's garb, tall and well built, but unemployed and thin. These young people could not get rations because they were neither aged, infirm, nor sick; there was no such thing as unemployment relief for aborigines. The soles of the young man's boots were worn through.

Next morning we set off in a T model Ford for Haast Bluff, just under two hundred miles to the westward, where we were to meet Pastor Albrecht and a camel convoy. The way lay north through the MacDonnell Ranges, then west. Three creeks had to be crossed, one of which, the Dashwood, was running. We experienced the greatest difficulty, after going through the water, in pushing the car over the steep farther bank. The last homestead we passed was in ruins, and the country about it sandy and windswept from overstocking and a prolonged drought. Beyond that the land, still then in the possession of aborigines, was in better heart.

Haast Bluff is a magnificent mountain. In the evening light it looks like a strong man lying on his back—chin, lips, mouth, nose, and forehead are all discernible. The changing appearance of the Bluff in the differing lights and shades was very impressive. More than a hundred naked tribal natives were at evening devotions with Pastor Albrecht as we drove up. Not one of them moved, although they knew of our coming, and had heard the car long before it arrived.

The aborigines at Haast Bluff were of two tribes—Pintubis from the Ehrenburg Range, and Gnalias from the Picilli Springs. The Pintubis had to leave the Ehrenburgs because the waterhole was damaged by interference; the Gnalias left their home when the Springs became part of a white man's cattle station. For two years there had been fighting between the tribes, but by 1936 it had ceased and they were living together along the Range. As the light faded, the women with the younger children returned to the family camp fires, but some time passed before the men and older boys joined them. I counted twenty-eight camp fires spread over a large area. Each aboriginal lay naked, with a low fire of hot embers on each side, and each family campsite was protected from the wind by a low windscreen made of brushwood. They were surrounded by warm air from the low camp fires that burned throughout the night, and so were not cold. But we on the ground, with blankets and rugs, were never warm.

Tribal mothers in the bush fondle their babies and croon to them just as white mothers do. In essentials there is no difference between aborigines and ourselves; fundamental joys and sorrows are common to both. Young children laugh and cry, play and gambol as our children do, and the older ones vary from the very intelligent to the dull, from the shy, sensitive child to the placid and less emotional type. The men too are like us; the majority active and lithe, but with the occasional lazy one. The great difference between the aborigines and ourselves lies in conditions of living. We have all the comforts and amenities of twentieth-century civilization; they have heat, and flies, and a hard battle every day to keep body and soul together.

Aboriginal men must be very fit, for it is their duty to hunt the large animals, the kangaroo, euro, wallaby, and emu. The women's job is to bring in the day's supply of vegetable food, yams, yelka, wapiti, nuts, fruits, berries, seeds, roots, and paraltja, sugar exudate from Eucalyptus leaves. They also collect honey ants, rabbits, witchetty grubs, goannas, and the smaller animals of the bush. The women set out early in the morning with digging-sticks and pitis, deep oval receptacles generally made of bark and fashioned by heat over the fire.

In drought times they cannot travel far from whatever water is available. The local food supply becomes less and less, and if the drought does not break, starvation is inevitable. This has happened in the past, but I have never heard of a national appeal being made to succour those aborigines in their distress. When an Independent Liberal member of Parliament in Western Australia, Mr W. Grayden, found in 1957 utterly appalling malnutrition among aborigines in the far eastern part of his State he brought the matter in story and photograph to public notice. Much sympathy was roused, and money contributed for immediate relief in the area. Nevertheless, considerable effort was made in certain official quarters to deny the seriousness of his report.

As guides on this trip we had two Aranda men, both of whom spoke English in addition to native languages. They also interpreted every mark on the ground. One forenoon we came on a lad of about twenty clothed in shirt, trousers, and boots. He had been in Alice Springs gaol till early in the year and when released walked two hundred miles to his home country. His offence was that he, a naked nomad, had been found in the bush eating a piece of bullock beef. He was put in chains, taken in for trial, and sentenced to six months' hard labour; but he escaped more than once and actually served a much longer period. There was no proof—I doubt if there was even a suggestion—that he had killed a bullock, but he was in possession of a piece of meat. In our law he would be an accessory after the fact; in tribal law it simply meant that in the traditional sharing of the carcass he was eating the piece allotted to him. The station owner has always demanded police protection of his bullocks, but what steps have been taken over the years to see that aborigines' interests would be safeguarded when bullocks eat up their vegetable food and frighten away their game?

A baby born at Haast Bluff a day or two before we arrived was still very light in colour. The palms of the hands and soles of the feet remain pale throughout life, but in a matter of weeks the face and body begin to darken.

One afternoon we watched the women preparing a meal from the seeds they had gathered earlier in the day. A middle-aged woman had a piti full of ega, grass seeds exactly like canary seed. Taking some of the seed in her left hand she worked her right fist against the seed. She kept repeating this, and as she shook the piti sharply the husks flew off in the breeze. Near by was a younger woman with an empty piti in front of her, and alongside it a piti with winnowed ega and a wooden dish with water. A large flat stone was inclined from the girl's knees on to the empty piti; on the stone some of the winnowed ega was placed and sprinkled with water. This was then ground by a round stone held in the woman's two hands. The wet flour-mass slid from the flat stone into the empty piti. This process went on until all the ega was moist flour in the piti. In another piti there was a supply of very fine reddish grass seeds. The two lots were mixed, and the resulting damper was laid on the hot ashes to cook.

Not far away was an old man breaking down native tobacco in his hand. The residue was mixed with fine ash and chewed. The resultant greenish quid was placed behind his left ear for later enjoyment. While at Haast Bluff we met four men who had been at Alice Springs, but had been induced by Pastor Albrecht to return to their tribal country. One of them, Ngunku, had been taken by police as a witness to Darwin from Mt Liebig two hundred miles west of Alice Springs and a thousand miles south of Darwin. Ngunku was held by the Police Department for six months until the trial was over. When a man is away from his tribe for any length of time another man must by tribal law care for his family, and if the husband returns after a long period there is the possibility of trouble. But Pastor Albrecht, Superintendent of Hermannsburg Mission, had for some years made camps in tribal country far removed from white civilization and put trained and trusted Aranda men in charge of them. The wife of Ngunku was cared for at one of these camps until her husband's return.

Every drop of water was precious on these camel journeys beyond settlement. On the evening we met these men we had soup for dinner, rice boiled in water which had previously boiled excess salt out of the salt beef! The second course, wallaby meat, was more palatable.

At Haast Bluff there was an outstanding Pintubi boy of about eleven years, Tjararu by name. I was told that in the shortest possible time he had picked up the Aranda language and now from me he learnt some English with a Scottish accent! He and I became friends at sight. Although not the oldest of the youngsters, Tjararu was the acknowledged leader of the group. It was his gift of perfect mimicry that first brought him to my notice. On rising after my first night on the ground, I was stiff, and stretched my arms in all directions. An hour or so after breakfast Tjararu, standing some distance away went through every action exactly as I had done. Cheeky? Not at all. We didn't know one another's language and this was his way of communicating with me. From that time we were firm friends, and when his tribe moved off he stayed behind with us. It was not easy to tell him he must follow his people, who had left the day before. How would he find them? I saw him walk over to the camp fire where his father, mother, and family had slept. Without stooping he picked up the footprints, and walking erectly he was soon lost to sight in the bush. This was his country, and he was exuberant with life, as was his splendid father. The outlook for these people seemed far from bright, for very, very few showed any concern for them. What happened to that country and its people will be told later.

On our last afternoon at Haast Bluff two men, an older and a younger, walked slowly towards us. Although the older man had a burn, still raw, on the right side of his neck, he was prop to his companion, a man of about twenty-four years. This young fellow was very weak from multiple sores and pulpy swellings in various parts of his body due to yaws. His pulse was 104. An arsenical preparation, N.A.B., the treatment for yaws before penicillin was discovered, was injected. After he had been given a period of rest one of the Aranda trained men, Gustav, took him on a donkey by easy stages to Hermannsburg, where he was given two further injections. When I saw him some weeks later he was full of smiles. Pastor Albrecht had done a splendid job in settling some of his finest Aranda men in country not then taken up by white settlers. These men in pairs were preparing the tribal aborigines for the contact with our civilization, which was inexorably creeping on them and for which the nation had made no effort to prepare them.

The majority of the boys I met at Haast Bluff had learnt our method of counting. Quite late one night I found out why. The boys were squatting around Gustav's camp fire asking him all sorts of questions about some of the knowledge he had acquired beyond their bush lore, and it was in this way he had taught them our numbers.

After four days at Haast Bluff we set off on camels, and I am not likely to forget that first day's ride! The day was windy, and I was riding with too short a stirrup. We crossed several creeks, climbed up steep banks, entered a mountain range, and crossed a steep, rock-strewn hill beyond which we decided to camp. After dismounting I lay flat on my back for half an hour without moving—too stiff to do anything else.

During the morning we had come on a large clay-pan covered with shallow water from recent rain. The evaporation rate is so high that the water does not lie very long. Pastor Albrecht said he had never before in his five years journeying in tribal country seen such an expanse of water, which resembled a lake while it lasted. The country all round was vivid with wild flowers and grass, and I remember especially one bush, a mass of scarlet berries. Soon after clearing the Haast Bluff Range—it is a two-day trip to the next rock hole—we travelled across red sandhills, dreary with spinifex and desert oaks. For miles every tree was dead from the prolonged severe drought.

This was my first experience of the long red sandhills, running more or less east and west, all parallel to one another and seemingly endless in number. It was depressing to ride up and down steep sandhills hour after hour with no sign of life on the ground or in the air. Aborigines cross this desert only in the winter time. After the interminable sand and dead trees we were glad to come on live desert oaks with their bright yellow tassel-like flowers welcoming us to somewhat better country, where we camped for the night.

Next day we crossed a grassy plain to the mountain range, and three hours riding along its base brought us to the mouth of a gorge. We followed the gorge for two miles until we came on Wotulpa, a deep rock hole lying at the foot of a great perpendicular rock-face. Here, seated by a fire and surrounded by pie melons they had gathered, were two aborigines who had passed us on the way. This was a memorable camp-site, for next day from the top of the mountain one could see range after range stretching into the far distance, and here and there salt-covered clay-pans from which white salt was blowing in the wind. Vividly I realized from that vantage point that in the dry Inland the good country is three or four miles out from the mountain ranges. Vegetable food and native game are plentiful there, and waterholes lie close to the mountains. It is in these parts the native tribes have lived since early times. Tragically for them it is just this good country that the white man covets for fattening his bullocks, and with one exception known to me has always obtained it.

There was much to see in the mountains. Rock wallabies were hopping about and leaping from ledge to ledge. Three of the highest ledges had been the nesting place of eagles. From any of these one could command the whole plain. I found no other place with a similar view. There were several large, deep waterholes on the mountains, and at the highest of these were the ashes of a native's little fire.

Back at camp the native guides had brought in a euro, the kind of kangaroo that lives on the mountain slopes. It has hair that is longer and coarser than the soft fur of the kangaroo. Kangaroo meat, incidentally, was certainly a welcome relief from the salt beef we had been having. Next day, after passing over the Wotulpa Range we travelled south in the direction of Mt Liebig across waterless country so poor that there was no feed for the camels, and the ground was so covered with spinifex that we had to burn off a patch to get enough room to lay out our swags. Again we had to cross seemingly interminable red sandhills for more than four hours, with only patches of spinifex to break the monotony. We were entirely dependent on our two natives for direction and for providing us with meat. Guns, rifles, and cartridges were in their keeping during the whole trip.

That night the hobbled camels travelled far in search of feed, and in the morning when the natives were away looking for them I walked to the most southerly point of the sandhills and discovered how very easy it is to get lost. But for signs of movement in the camp I doubt if I could have found it. We were still two days' journey from water, and in washing up our dishes we used water in which potatoes were boiled the night before! There could be no washing of any kind until we reached the next waterhole.

Two days later in the afternoon we rode clear of sandhills and spinifex, and entered good country close to another range of mountains. Without our native guides we would have been hopelessly lost, but they took us unerringly through a gorge and along a creek to Ayantji waterhole. This is the centre from which two Hermannsburg natives made contact with the tribal aborigines over a wide area. Titus and Gustav were often away from this depot for weeks at a time, but no native ever stole anything from the store that was built there. When they worked, however, from another centre—Potati—a white man burst open the lockers and took all the food. Twenty-five miles is a long day's ride for heavily laden camels, and they were tired, as we were, when we made camp at half-past seven.

After breakfast next morning we stretched out in relaxation and admired Mt Liebig rearing its head behind a high range of mountains and looking out over the great plain we had crossed the day before. But in the afternoon we were on our way again. The sun was very hot; there was not a breath of wind, not a cloud in the sky, not a sound except the clinking of hobble chains, and for the first time we rode without overcoats. Even in mid-winter the sun can be too warm for comfort in the interior of Australia. At last, away towards the south, a long strip of cloud appeared. It rose higher and higher, and eventually covered the sky; when it shut out the sun travelling became more comfortable. Still moving west between the mountain ranges we reached Warren Creek and made our camp there.

That night we were listening to orchestral music from Adelaide. Even in 1936 the miracle of wireless made it possible for us in tribal country in the heart of Australia to hear music more than a thousand miles away. Pastor Albrecht had with him one of the very earliest of Alf Traeger's wonderful pedal wireless sets. What these sets did for the security and comfort of the outback can never be overestimated.

Next day we set out for Potati, or Mt Peculiar as it appears on the map. The older of our two guides knew this country and went off with the gun in search of game, while Pastor Albrecht, confident of knowing the way, continued his happy practice of reading as he rode on the camel. But in less than an hour we realized that we were travelling with more hope than assurance! It was well into the afternoon before we found a "pad," a narrow, well-worn track made by animals going to water. This we followed to the waterhole, where our camels got their first drink for eighteen days—as far as we knew.

With his boots on, our guide who had gone hunting had been unsuccessful early in the day, but barefooted in the late afternoon he shot three kangaroos, and we were glad to have meat again. Potati was an interesting water-soak at the side of the hill with a small deep pool scooped out a little way from it. This had probably been made by the natives, and they had arranged two covers, one of bush and one of rocks from which to spear kangaroos and emus that came in the evening to drink.

Far to the west could be seen the Ehrenburg Range, scene of a near tragedy when T. G. H. Strehlow and two aborigines nearly perished some years before. They had gone to the once permanent waterhole at Ilbili, and found it dry. Somebody, perhaps with the idea of enlarging its capacity, had damaged it irretrievably. Strehlow told me that this experience was one of the worst he had had during his many years as a patrol officer.

Sixty miles north of Ilbili lay Mt Davenport with the Picilli Springs. These used to be the centre of Gnalia cultural and spiritual life, and the tribe's chief corroboree ground. Picilli is heard of in all the main myths and legends of the tribe. Now the springs water the white man's cattle, and the Gnalia people are scattered far and wide. We had met some of them at Haast Bluff, some were wandering on the MacDonnell Ranges, some had gone to Coniston cattle station, and some were at Ryan's Well. Separated from their age-long home, the heritage of their fathers, the tribe found its sanctions weakened, and they faced inevitable detribalization. They, like thousands of their kin in other parts of Australia, would drift in to the settled areas there to scrounge for the barest subsistence and to be despised. It is damnable that year after year land capable of fattening sheep or cattle has been lost to its original owners without recompense to them ever being considered.

In the United States of America in August, 1946, an Indian Claims Commission was set up "to hear and determine claims against the United States on behalf of any Indian tribe, band or other indefinable group of American Indians residing within the United States." One of the clauses was for "claims arising from the taking by the United States whether as the result of a treaty of cession or otherwise of lands owned or occupied by the claimant without the payment of compensation agreed to by the claimant."

No Government in Australia has ever considered compensation of aboriginal tribes. Instead, year after year, as the white man has moved in from the coast the tribes have been dispossessed, and, where they could not be exploited, regarded as a nuisance. Little wonder that the late Professor Wood Jones referred to us as having the mark of Cain on our brow.

4

Myall Travelling Companions

THE REST AT Potati, with ample water and fresh game, gave
us renewed vigour to tackle another day's crossing of sandhills
which make for such dreary and difficult going. We camped late,
dead tired after our hottest day. The night was warm, the sky
overcast and threatening rain. When rain falls, camel-travelling
must stop and all saddles have to be put under tarpaulin. Saddles
if wet are too heavy for the camels, and the only way to dry a
saturated saddle is to take it to pieces, dry the straw, repack
it and sew on the leather covering. It is easier to wait until the
rain stops, and quicker too. A hold-up could be serious if
one were camped away from water; near to a waterhole it would
be merely a matter of some discomfort and loss of time. But
fortunately the night passed without rain, and breakfast found
us enjoying a delicious omelette made from an emu's egg. In
one of these there is enough for six people.

Soon after setting out again we met three tribal men, all
in outstanding physical condition. Katinkura, a man of about
thirty-four, had with him two younger men, an Ilbili man, and
a man from the Kintore Range near the border of Western
Australia. Katinkura had two wives and three children. Pastor
Albrecht gave to each man and woman a piece of kangaroo
meat as a goodwill offering. Australian aborigines share
everything with their fellows, and as we were in aboriginal tribal
land we followed their custom.

The whole party travelled with us throughout the day. The
men usually walked well ahead of the women and to the right.
The two elder children were lifted on to Pastor Albrecht's camel,
where the older child, aged about three, perched herself fearlessly
on the swag on the forward part of the saddle. The younger
one on the Pastor's left knee snuggled into his side and was
soon fast asleep. In the afternoon the Ilbili man speared a

rabbit. From my camel I saw him throw the spear and afterwards toss the rabbit to Katinkura, who a few minutes later slit open the abdomen, threw away the entrails and sewed up the rent with a piece of sharp mulga twig. It was later given to the women and children for their evening meal.

For the greater part of the day we rode through thick mulga scrub, and at times had to bend down sharply to avoid being jabbed in the face by dead, stiff spikes. Again our evening camp was in red sand and spinifex—two nights out from Potati soak with little water remaining in our leather water-carriers. The native party camped near us, Katinkura leaving the men's fire and joining his family, where each individual slept between two slow-burning little fires. In the morning they broke camp almost in seconds. Katinkura spoke to his wives, picked up his spears and woomera, and the women quickly collected their digging sticks and pitis. Each wife slung a child on her shoulder, and they were off on the trail, the husband moving to the right to join the other men. This interesting group, with their one dog, a pure-bred dingo used for hunting, were soon lost to us.

We on the other hand were delayed because our camels, though hobbled, had wandered far in search of food. Our native camel-man was away for three and a half hours before he brought them in, and it was eleven o'clock before we got away. Travelling past Mangeraka mountain we reached Halcomb's Creek late in the afternoon and an hour later met the group of aborigines who had come south from Haast Bluff to meet us.

The water here was got by digging in the sandy creek bed and ladling it out. The natives had already made a good "soak" in this way as they had been here two days. Even donkeys knew the trick; one of them was scraping aside the sand with its hoof and drinking after each scraping. The aborigines told us that brumbies, wild horses, do the same when surface water is not available.

Among this group of aborigines was my young friend Tjararu and two of his mates. He greeted me with a "good-day" and had not forgotten my name—but he had donned some cast-off clothing. What a sad contrast to the fine alert appearance of these same boys in their natural naked state. Next day Tjararu and his friend Warangula presented me with two young emus. I was in a dilemma: I knew I should accept the gift, but what on earth could I do with two live baby emus? After thanking the boys very warmly I persuaded them to keep the birds for their own breakfast. I think they understood.

That morning the ground was white with frost, and the water we had left in our washbasin was solid ice. One has to be physically fit to travel in the country beyond settlement. New kinds of food, many different sources of water, as well as prolonged exposure to the elements, with extremes of temperature, can all cause trouble. One of our party, David Munro, could not take breakfast, and I found he had a high temperature, but he insisted on carrying on. He was under treatment for the next four days, was very weak, and wobbled in the saddle. Each evening he went thankfully to bed the moment the camels were "hooshed" and I had laid out his swag.

On our last evening at this waterhole Pastor Albrecht gave a devotional talk to the native folk, who then went off over the hill, each with his fire-stick. It was a picturesque sight. They waved the sticks aloft as they went over the top together, and almost immediately afterwards the hillside burst into flame from bottom to top. The men had fired the clumps of spinifex as they went; the spinifex was green at that time of the year and took fully a minute or two to flare up. It was from burning the spinifex that the natives got the black resin which they used for hafting the flint to the woomera and other tools.

In the morning before we left I spoke to the people—the younger Hermannsburg guide interpreting for me. It was interesting to watch the attentive faces and to hear "awa, awa" as they nodded assent to some of my points. I have nothing but the happiest memories of these fine people, and the more I came to know them individually the more determined I became to work for their recognition as citizens of Australia. They gave us a great send off, and seemed to feel the parting keenly. So did we.

That day's travel was especially memorable for the beauty of scenery we met with in the late afternoon. We passed through a mountain gap whose walls were gorgeously coloured as the sun caught the rocks, and riding through another gap we came on a good camping-place among the mulga in a narrow valley. After the evening meal, a dead tree—roots, trunk, and branches—was laid on the hot embers and soon the whole length of the tree was aglow. I was able to write up my diary by its light.

Next day saw our return to occupied country as we passed through Glen Helen Station—17,000 square miles. It was the

Primitive tribal aborigines. Women and babies, Petermann Ranges.

Group of men from Pitjantjatjara tribe. Lalili in middle looking round.

Namatjira in 1934, two years before he started painting. He cut mulga logs in the bush, sliced them, and did poker-work on the slices

Housing of part-whites at Copley, South Australia.

first time since leaving Alice Springs that we had seen cattle. There was great contrast between the herbage of the natural country of the aborigines and the country overrun by cattle. One white man with his herds can render impossible the health and happiness of two hundred aborigines.

"The Roof of Australia," as Pastor Albrecht called the MacDonnell Ranges, was crossed the following afternoon, and now we were in the tribal country of our main native guide, of his father, and of his grandfather. He had been an unfailing and never-doubting guide; to his knowledge of several aboriginal languages he added an intimate understanding of the language of the ground—reading tracks as though they were the pages of a book. On one occasion he told us from footprints at a rock hole the name of the man who had been there. Another time we came on a windbreak and burnt out fires between which men had slept. He named the men, told us how laden with skins they had been, and in which direction they had gone. He correctly judged which day they were likely to reach Hermannsburg. And all this was read, easily, from an erect position.

On these nights in our swags on the ground we looked up at the moon and myriads of stars in a cloudless sky, with not even the faintest breeze to break the almost desolate calm. In the mornings the water in our basins had to be melted before we could have breakfast.

Each day brought us nearer to our destination, Hermannsburg. On our last morning, with a view to an early start, our younger guide left camp before daybreak to bring in the camels. But when he returned three hours later he had only five of them. The older guide on his riding camel followed camel tracks in the opposite direction, and after two and a half hours came back with the other five. So it was nearly midday when we got the camels loaded; two hours later we stopped for lunch, our last bush meal, in the dry river bed of the Finke. We boiled our billy near to the hut of a full-blood boundary rider. He had a well-made wurlie, an excellent butcher's hut, a goat yard with a separate enclosure for kids. There was tragedy here; his wife was very ill with pulmonary tuberculosis and had suffered a severe haemorrhage just before we arrived. We did what little we could for her.

We received a joyful welcome at Hermannsburg in the late afternoon. A stream of children led by Pastor Albrecht's Helen,

Theodore, and Paul, came running to meet us in great excitement. With my three weeks' growth of rust-red beard I was unrecognizable and there was much laughter over Mrs Albrecht's not knowing me until I spoke! It was agony to remove that beard but hot baths were ready for us, followed by a meal which was a real feast after three weeks of bush "tucker."

The desert sand at Hermannsburg was blossoming "like the rose" since the coming of the water from Koporilya, the hillside spring three miles away. Officialdom had not encouraged this water-scheme, but the Hermannsburg natives under the guidance of Pastor Albrecht carried it through, with the result that vegetables of every description were growing in abundance. The contrast in the appearance of the people, especially the children, with that of two years before was very noticeable. The demolition of the tuberculosis-infected huts by the old men has already been mentioned, and no doubt this also was a strong contributing factor to the new look of health and happiness at the Mission.

The eighty-mile truck drive back to Alice Springs brought us near the end of our trip, and we were soon on the train travelling home to the south. On the train with us was an octoroon, J.B., who had been working on a cattle station. He had a long-standing and severe infection of both eyes, but there was at that time no hospital at Alice Springs nor any place where a sick person with any aboriginal blood could go for medical care. He was being sent down to the Royal Adelaide Hospital.

There was an interesting follow-up to this camel trip with Pastor Albrecht. On my return I got in touch with the Minister for the Interior, the Hon T. Paterson, and pointed out the need to make the Haast Bluff area a reserve for aborigines to save the Pintubi and Gnali tribes who had settled there. The Minister was sympathetic and said that if a report by his Senior Patrol Officer agreed with my report he would act. He told me later that his officer had agreed with me, but in January, 1937, in Alice Springs a white man secured a licence to open a cattle station in that very country. I wired the Minister and saw him the following day, when he assured me he would certainly honour his promise. All grazing licences in the Haast Bluff area were terminated, and later eight thousand square miles were declared an aboriginal reserve. The history of this reserve is recorded in a publication issued in 1961 by the Welfare Branch of the Northern Territory Administration. It is good to remember that once at least the white man's interests came second to the aborigines' need.

I was asked on my return from the Interior about an alleged spear attack by "natives in war-paint." I reported there was no sign of unrest in the country adjoining the Central Reserve, in which at that time two expeditions were said to be scouting. One of them was making a film. It turned out that the so-called war-painted natives were aborigines who had been painted by an unauthorized film party, and that some time later these men had been sighted from the air by the other party who were looking for Lasseter's Gold Reef in the Reserve. The Federal Government, it is believed, confiscated eight thousand feet of film when it reached Sydney. I also gave it as my opinion that Lasseter's Reef was a myth, and that trespassing on the Reserve to the detriment of the aborigines had increased because of the publicity given to the story.

My happy experience with tribal aborigines in their own country made me very conscious of the sad contrast between that life and life for aborigines on cattle stations. In this regard I was deeply shocked to read in Western Australian *Hansard,* No. 11, 1936, of the utterly callous attitude of some of the members of the Legislative Council in Western Australia to aboriginal women on cattle stations.

On a Bill for an Aborigines Act Amendment the trend of discussion was to minimize the penalty for white men on cattle stations in the North having sexual intercourse with aboriginal women. Youth was not to be "unduly penalized for what might happen because of his inexperience!" The offence was one "that amounts merely to obeying a natural law or impulse." "There is a tendency for young men to refuse to go into the back country. We know the difficulty of getting white men to go there, and a severe strain is being inflicted upon the people who are there." "I am concerned about the development of the back country." "This is a Bill to protect the aborigines," said the Chief Secretary; but another member said "It would not be too much to suggest that we take steps to sterilize these unfortunate young women," presumably against the results of what another member called "a casual offence by a young fellow." Finally an Hon member who had moved an amendment withdrew it, as he had been given to understand that "it is not so much a matter of protecting aboriginal women from white men as of protecting white men from disease." What unmitigated humbug, when we know that aboriginal women did not suffer from these venereal diseases until infected by white men; and in many cases became sterile as a result.

In September of 1936 the General Assembly of the Presbyterian Church of Australia met in Sydney. At the Mission evening session I showed slides of the aborigines I had met in 1934 and the two following years, and next day moved on behalf of the Board of Missions, that the Church should undertake a mission to aborigines in the Musgrave Ranges. In order to stimulate interest in the project I had already attended the State Presbyterian Assemblies in Victoria, New South Wales, and South Australia—all in this same year—and had given reasons for the choice of Ernabella as the ideal site. Between it and the Great Central Aborigines Reserve of 65,000 square miles there were three "doggers."

With the establishment of the Mission which would ensure for the natives the regular Government subsidy for dingo scalps I felt sure the "doggers" would go. The mission would then be in close contact with the last of the tribal aborigines in South Australia.

The motion was finally passed, and this meant that the whole Presbyterian Church of Australia accepted responsibility for the venture.

5

Camel Patrol

IT WAS TEN years since I had been to my home in Scotland, and in 1937 I returned in order to do further post-graduate study, and to take my wife and children to see my father, who was then still living in Ayrshire. Knowing of my plans, the Moderator General, Dr John Mackenzie, had nominated me to represent the Presbyterian Church of Australia at Oxford at a forthcoming Ecumenical Conference on "Church, Community and State." He asked me to speak on Church and Race with special reference to Australian aborigines. This I did, and the finding of the Commission on this issue was clear —

> There is no room for any differentiation between the races as to their intrinsic value. All share alike in the concern of God, being created by Him to bring their unique and distinctive contribution to His service in the world. The sin of man asserts itself in racial pride, racial hatred and persecution and in the exploitation of other races. Against this in all its forms the Church is called by God to set its face implacably and to utter its word unequivocally, both within and without its own borders.
>
> In the services of worship, in its organization and in the hospitality of the Christian home there can be no place for seclusion or segregation because of race or colour. To allow the Church's line of action to be determined by racial discrimination denies the Gospel whose proclamation is its task and commission.

My speaking at this Conference gave some of the delegates their first knowledge that we had any coloured people in Australia at all. And I found this ignorance of our aborigines fairly general throughout the Old Country. So it is understandable that much interest was aroused by an illustrated address I gave a few months later in London for the Anti-Slavery and Aborigines Protection Society. The lecture was at the Royal Empire Society, London, and Professor Gilbert Murray, O.M., was in the chair. At its conclusion Professor Murray startled the audience with some grim reminiscences of early pioneering days in Australia. His father had at one time owned a station, and unlike so many of his fellows had shown respect and care for aborigines. Others had regarded them as vermin to be exterminated as quickly as possible. Professor Murray told of the pitiful cries of aborigines dying of poisoned flour.

This lecture, with a number of my slides reproduced, was given much publicity in the press. My statement that no clear Government policy existed to save aborigines, and that the public of Australia were not interested enough to force the issue, was supported by Professor Wood Jones, F.R.S. In Melbourne he said:

> No Australian Government has ever had any desire to preserve the native race. Unless something is done to move the public and the Governments in 30 years Australia will be indelibly branded with the brand of Cain.

A few weeks later in Canberra Dr Donald Thomson, Anthropologist of Melbourne University, said:

> I have come south from Arnhem Land completely discouraged because of the unresponsiveness of the administration, its failure to frame a policy of native administration, and its apparent ignorance of its responsibilities to the aborigines.

Confirming these opinions a statement in *The Northern Standard,* 20 August 1937, came from Matthew Thomas, who had been a ganger in charge of a native road-repairing gang on Wave Hill cattle station in the Northern Territory.

> For ten weeks I was in charge of a gang of natives repairing the road for over 100 miles between Wave Hill and Inverway Station. My gang consisted of three boys [men] and seven lubras. They worked exceptionally well with pick, shovels, bars upon the roads and with axes in felling trees and cutting bushes. . . .

The job was eventually finished to the satisfaction of the Wave Hill Management. The native wages were: plenty of beef, damper, tea, sugar with three sticks of dried up nicky tobacco for each boy, and two sticks for each lubra per week. Trousers, shirts, and boots were sent out for the boys, but nothing for the lubras, who had to make dresses from flour bags to cover their naked bodies. They worked harder and longer hours than the bucks. That the natives were working under slave conditions cannot be disputed, also that they worked under appalling conditions with the sanction and approval of the Minister of Territory Affairs and the Chief Protector of Aboriginals. From personal observations the working conditions of the Wave Hill natives is no better and no worse than those upon other stations throughout the Territory and the East and West Kimberleys. . . .

In their minds and hearts these people of colour resent the white man's injustice and indifference to better standards of living for them in a white man's civilisation. . . .

No reasonable man with a sense of justice and fair play can honestly deny the Australian native and half-caste the right to live under more humane conditions in their own country.

No comment need be added to these statements of fact except to say that the "Minister for Territory Affairs" means the Minister responsible for the Northern Territory. The title "Minister for Territories" was a much later portfolio.

In 1939 the Federal Government became very much perturbed at the large number of tribal aborigines who in the previous year or two had settled on cattle stations between the Central Aboriginal Reserve and Alice Springs.

To find out why this was taking place T. G. H. Strehlow, then Deputy-Chief Protector of Aborigines in the Northern Territory, was instructed to visit the Petermann Range in the Reserve to ascertain the food conditions, vegetable and game, and to estimate the number of aborigines there and their state of health. Strehlow considered the trip too risky for one truck, and I was asked to join the Protector and Pastor Albrecht of

Hermannsburg with the Ernabella Mission truck driven by the Superintendent, the Rev Harry Taylor.

In past trips I had found the Inland parched, but not so this year. From Marree to Oodnadatta on the way north, and on to the Finke, water was lying on both sides of the railway, and washaways were frequent. We reached the Finke siding to learn that the Ernabella truck was bogged twenty-eight miles out, and this in mid-winter, when rain is not expected in the Interior. That night we slept in a railway fettler's cottage, and next morning, the truck having got through to us, we set off for the Musgrave Ranges. We were soon in trouble. The ground was so soft that we took four hours to cover the first twenty-five miles, the truck being bogged to the axles three times. Two full days passed before we completed the two hundred miles to the Musgrave Ranges, where the Ernabella Mission was now established.

The next two days were mainly occupied with Harry Taylor making a careful overhaul of the truck, which had been subjected to such a battering between the railway siding and Ernabella. We were anxious also to try out thoroughly the new and powerful radio set which had been generously provided for our patrol by the South Australian weekly paper *Radio Call*. Having failed to make contact with Broken Hill, the northern station, I unwittingly broke all the rules by speaking direct to Adelaide! The resulting telegram from my wife more than compensated for the severe though courteous rebuke received from Broken Hill for our interference. Broken Hill then took our wave-length and gave us official status as 8YM Patrol. This powerful patrol set, which at that time was Alfred Traeger's latest, was to prove invaluable to us in the next three weeks of arduous patrol through the Musgrave and Petermann Ranges to the Western Australian border.

T. G. H. Strehlow and Pastor Albrecht arrived next day by truck from Hermannsburg, and at once we started sorting stores for the trip and loading up. It was late the following morning when the two trucks moved off, heading north through the Musgraves. During the afternoon we halted at a soak where it was known that a white man had camped the previous winter and had collected dingo scalps from tribal aborigines. An hour later we came to a most unusual rock formation, great blocks of rock that looked to be larger than the stones of the Pyramids piled high on the steep slope of the mountain. It was hard to imagine why they did not crash to the ground.

On reaching Michell's Nob, an outstanding peak, on the northern side of the Range we turned west, and later that day we had a view of the lonely monolith, Mt Connor. We travelled close to the mountains until we reached the western end of the Range, from where we could see Ayers Rock and Mt Olga in the distance. Going north-west we passed the many individual mountains that lie between the Musgrave and the Petermann Ranges.

Rocks soon became so frequent and so large that it seemed almost impossible for the trucks to proceed. After a reconnaissance we set off with great care, and by driving slowly negotiated the defiles and soon afterwards camped for the night. The following day's travel along the base of Foster's Cliff among rocks and boulders was so difficult that Strehlow decided to change our route: leave the mountains and drive across the sandhills to Piltardi Rock Hole at the eastern end of the Petermanns. Although sandhills are generally regarded as a hazard for trucks, we actually found the going much easier and reached Piltardi before sunset.

As we jumped from the trucks in the fading light we saw by the glare of a small fire a naked tribal father and son sitting by it. Strehlow was especially cheered as he realized this man could prove to be the guide we would need on the camel trip through his tribal country. The camels from the Hermannsburg Mission were waiting for us here—six riding and six pack camels —with their aboriginal riders. This was to be our base camp from now on.

The conditions on the truck trip had not turned out as expected. A three year drought had broken a month before we set out, and contrary to our expectations the sandy stretches provided better travelling than the country nearer the ranges, where the wheels at times made ruts six inches deep and for most of the way the heavy three-ton truck was doing only four miles to the gallon. We were often in bottom gear, and never in top. From time to time as the heat of the day increased tyres had to be deflated, and frequent stops were made to allow the engines to cool. The staking of tyres had proved serious.

Travelling due west in the late afternoon, the drivers had been dazzled by the setting sun and even at a slow pace were unable to see snags on the ground. The country we had passed through varied greatly; though sand was predominant there were tracts of country with desert oaks, corkwood, and ironwood trees and occasional kurrajongs. At times we would pass through thick mulga, then through patches of dead and fallen timber, at one time so thick we had to clear the ground by hand. Sometimes the grass was high, at other times dead buck-bush had banked up on the ground; we also drove through wide plains of spinifex. We had crossed many dry creek beds, some deep, narrow, and stony; some wide and sandy.

Half-way between the two ranges Strehlow had taken stock of the petrol supply; we had held a consultation and agreed to continue until half our supply was used. The first thing done on arrival at Piltardi was to check the petrol—seventy-nine gallons had been used, eighty remained!

Our first day at Piltardi was spent on overhauling the trucks and sorting out goods for the camel trip ahead. Then everyone had a bath; clothes were washed and easily dried before night in a good wind and strong sun. Before setting off along the Petermann Range Strehlow was anxious to try out the camels, and he arranged that the guide Tjuintjara and his boy should take us southward of the main range to Lasseter's grave, a day's journey.

All the aborigines along the Petermanns were myalls, tribal naked nomads untouched by civilization. In the day's travelling we did not see any native game. And Tjuintjara told us that many of his people had died of starvation the year before, 1938. But now the long drought was past and there were signs of life: fresh young gum leaves iridescent in the breeze, the call of the bell-bird, and bright green parrots on the wing. At one place Tjuintjara saw bush cucumbers in a tree, and brought them down with the barb of his spear.

At three-thirty we reached Lasseter's grave, a terribly desolate spot, and the whole range here was most forbidding. To this place the unconscious and dying Lasseter had been carried by tribal aborigines who found him in a cave further west. He died here in the rough shelter they built round him, and was later buried by Bob Buck, the settler to whom the aborigines had gone many miles for help. A few hours' riding brought us back to the base camp, and a good fire, with tea ready for us.

Next day we set out on our camel patrol with Tjuintjara guiding us; he had sent his son off to his mother to let her know where her husband was going. Our first night's camp was in the Casterton Creek, and by the following afternoon we had crossed the Irvine and were halted at the Shaw River bed to look for water, which we found close to the mountain two miles in from the plain. Strehlow was anxious to find out if it would be possible to get the camels through the gorge to the southern side of the Range. So he set off with Pastor Albrecht and Harry Taylor to assess the chances, while I lay down in the dry creek bed and fell fast asleep. In an hour they returned to say they thought it was possible we might get across.

It proved just possible! It was a difficult climb, and nearing the top of the mountain Strehlow and his faithful full-blood Tom, who was in charge of the camels, went ahead to have a closer look at the position. No white man had ever before been across the Petermanns by this route. They found that without some preparatory work we could go no further. With Tom and Tjuintjara, Strehlow dispatched dead timber and dislodged boulders into the gorge hundreds of feet below. We were then told to proceed slowly in single file on this narrow path, each of us leading his riding camel in order to minimize the danger as we rounded the hairpin bends. I have always disliked heights, and was very wary as I went ahead and inched my way round, keeping my eyes fixed on the rock face until I was safely across. By dusk we were all over the top, and an hour later camped for the night on a high plateau. Rain fell soon afterwards but not for long.

The next day's travel was bitterly cold as we made our way over a mulga plateau surrounded by hills. By late afternoon we had reached Pitulu water-soak at the end of the plateau about twelve miles south of the summit of the Petermanns, crossed late the day before. Looking south from the top of a hill we could see the Mann Range in South Australia some fifty miles away. As far as the eye could see the country was a plain of mulga and spinifex, with sandhills. As we left this hill we saw a huge eagle's next and noticed too the footmarks of wild turkeys. But although there were occasional tracks of emus and kangaroos we did not sight game or people.

Our night's camp was made at O'Kulka waterhole, and by wireless at seven-thirty we were setting our watches by the

Adelaide G.P.O. clock and soon afterwards were listening-in to a symphony concert from the Sydney Town Hall. There was opposition to the orchestra: from curlews piping in the bush! It was the coldest, clearest of nights, with myriads of stars in the deep blue sky, and when we rose at dawn the ground and the tarpaulins that covered us were white with frost. The day was cold, and Tjuintjara, native-wise, fired a clump of spinifex to light his fire-stick, which he carried with him for warmth. The camels too felt the cold and seemed very nervous during the afternoon. Camels, especially the younger ones, are said to have a hatred of going far from home, and we were now not far from the West Australian border.

As we made camp that night there was an incident which might have proved serious. When the camel with the Ernabella water canteens was down being unloaded it rose suddenly, with the two metal canteens dangling under its belly and in the way of its legs. It was still roped to another camel, and soon both were thoroughly frightened and started tearing about with the water camel lashing at the canteens. In a moment all twelve camels were on their feet, snorting and plunging wildly about, making each of us in turn duck for safety. Eventually somebody was able to grasp a rope hanging from the camel in trouble, and we all hung on to it.

Holding a sharp bush knife, I went forward to cut the rope, when there was a wild yell from the others as a flying hind foot just missed my head. But I was on the alert and at the second attempt managed to slash the rope. That brought one canteen to the ground, with the other sliding but still dangling between the camel's legs. The poor beast, terribly frightened, lashed out in all directions; its hind legs were badly cut and it was impossible to use it for the rest of the trip.

Getting the team hooshed again, unloaded, and hobbled, was a very ticklish job. They were thoroughly rattled, and when freed at the edge of the camp they hopped off with amazing vigour in spite of their hobbles. There was more trouble to come. During the upset the pot filled with stew for our evening meal had boiled dry; somebody added cold water, and the pot cracked with a loud report. We were hungry and hoped that the spilt mash would be eatable, but it was not. We found some relief from the situation in a hearty laugh.

The night was again very cold and the ground covered with frost when we woke in the morning. We were now so far west that dawn came late; there was only the faintest glimmer of light in the eastern sky at six-forty. Lunchtime on this day was spent in the Hull River bed, alongside the cave where Lasseter had spent his last two months.

Lasseter had floated a company in the South to mine what he claimed was a gold-bearing reef in the Petermann Ranges. From Alice Springs trucks and aeroplanes sallied forth, but the reef, if ever it existed, was never found. The disillusioned members of the party returned home, but Lasseter with a mate stayed on. Before long his mate also left and Lasseter was alone. Had he accepted the proffered help of the aborigines he would not have perished; but he was afraid of them and fired his rifle in the air whenever they approached. So they left him alone, and it was only when his strength was failing that he is said to have fired once again—this time perhaps to attract attention. Naturally, however, the aborigines did not interfere until all firing ceased. When they approached and finally entered the cave Lasseter was too weak to rise. He could swallow water, but little else. Recognizing his plight as serious the aborigines set off to carry him to the nearest cattle station, a long distance away, but as we have seen, he died on the way.

I photographed the cave from the outside, and from the inside to find what Lasseter had looked out on. The cave swarmed with small flies, and when I came out I was covered with them. Thirty yards from the cave there was a good soak in the bed of the river, and from there Lasseter must have got his water. We were out of water, and Strehlow at once dug a deep hole. There were shells on the walls of the hole, and it was interesting to watch the water trickling from the side nearer the cave. Twenty gallons were needed and it took about two and a half hours to fill our canteens.

Leaving Lasseter's cave and still travelling westwards we came on a large circular area in which all the trees had been snapped off at ground level; the result, probably, of a powerful willy-willy or whirlwind. From here we passed through much dead timber, but later through beautiful Petermann wattles, desert oaks, mallee, and mulga scrub. Spinifex-covered sandhills were much in evidence later in the day. No game was seen, nor any sign of human life, except for some old tracks of a camel-buggy, which were evidence of intruders in the Aborigines Reserve.

On waking next morning I saw Tjuintjara sitting by the embers that had kept him warm all night. Over the fire he was heating a long spear shaft, and then manipulating it with his hands and teeth to get it perfectly straight. Without his knowing it I took a photograph of him from my swag a few yards away. All that morning we rode among sandhills, but in the afternoon came upon beautiful eucalypts with pure white trunks—the ghost gums—and rounding a bluff of the Petermanns we saw the spectacular spur from the main range, imaginatively named "The Ruined Ramparts." Later still we came to a gap for which we had been anxiously looking and halted on the bank of the Docker River.

This was our first warm day; the trip had been strenuous, and we were all feeling the strain. Although there were birds about we had not found water there and Tjuintjara said he was sure he did not know any more rock holes further west. It was clear that he was not happy about travelling any further from his home country. The day before, he had seen strange footprints on the sand, and as tribal aborigines know the footprints of all their own folk, he was alarmed at finding these unknown ones. During the night he had cried out in nightmare—as we all do under stress—I was sleeping only a few yards from him.

6

Return From The West

SEEING OUR GUIDE'S reluctance to venture further Strehlow
explained to him that we had planned to return as soon as our
water supply was replenished. Tjuintjara then became a
different man; cheery and happy and in no doubt about the route
to water even though it was still a little westwards! So we
struck camp and left the Docker River, in good heart for our
short final ride to the west. About half a mile north-west of our
camp we saw a powerful willy-willy which hurled a column of
sand twenty feet into the air and sent dry buck-bush up at least
three hundred feet! On our way we rode among huge trees which
during a bush fire had been blackened to a height of twenty feet
—good reason for not travelling in summer. And now the
twittering of waxbills cheered us, and quite suddenly we came
on a splendid waterhole, the finest water since our base camp at
Piltardi.

Camels were watered, canteens filled, and bread and damper
made for the homeward trip. After that came the washing of
clothes and the luxury of a bath. As I was last on the "roster"
for use of the big dish which served each one of us for a bath, I
climbed one of the near-by heights to have a look at the mountains in Western Australia. Taking what I thought to be careful
stock of my surroundings, I continued to climb height after
height, and when ready to turn back found I could not see the
camp. Deciding on a certain direction, I came after a time on
old camel-buggy tracks and followed them to the waterhole. I
had gone about two-thirds of a circle from the place where I
set out, proving that one should never go anywhere in the bush
without an aboriginal companion.

Soon after we had settled our camp two tribal men walked
towards us—the first people we had seen since leaving the
Musgraves. After a talk with Strehlow and Pastor Albrecht

63

they left, but soon returned with their womenfolk, followed by another myall, a fine, upstanding young man with wife and child, and an old woman. It was their misfortune that they had recently "sold" their dingo scalps to two white men, the owners of the camel-buggy whose tracks we had crossed. These natives seemed happy, and looked healthy and in good condition, although they said there was very little game about. During the trip we ourselves had seen neither kangaroos nor emus, and only one dingo.

Strehlow, as Protector, reported by wireless to Perth the camel-buggy tracks in the Reserve, and later we heard that two white "doggers" returning to civilization were fined. Unfortunately the small sum imposed would be a negligible amount compared with the considerable sums they would gain from their trading with the natives for dingo scalps.

Before starting for home next day we prepared rations for this little group of aborigines who would be travelling with us and so would be unable to hunt for food. And then we were on our way, with a pause for lunch in the midst of the most beautiful ghost gums and in view of the impressive Ruined Ramparts. Lunch over, we made for a gap in the mountains to make our way through to the northern side of the range. The going was very rocky, and only camels could have crossed here, as was the case in many other places on the patrol. Here at the foot of the mountain was a waterhole, at which all the natives drank. It was probably permanent water as near by there was an old camping ground with many windbreaks. Clear of the range we turned right and were soon crossing sandhills again. Away to our left a small fire was seen; a call came through the bush and was answered by Tjuintjara who ran over to the fire.

Here was an old man who came across and joined us. Half an hour later we saw several more fires and we were soon joined by a family party. One of the two natives who had first walked into our camp a few days earlier had gone off and brought in this group of nine people, including two babies on the breast. There was, too, a youth in the offing, walking on the left and always well ahead and away from the rest of the natives. There was a reason for his segregation.

Strehlow was anxious to push on to the Hull River before stopping, as we had noticed on the way that there was plenty of young buck-bush—good camel feed. So it was nearly seven

Man brought in to Oodnadatta from a northern cattle station.

Dead desert oaks in the dry heart of Australia.

Water-soak in the Petermann Ranges.

Woman carrying water from rock hole in piti. Petermann Ranges.

o'clock when we halted, all very tired, and that included the camels too. We had been travelling too fast.

My first job on dismounting was always to start the fire. This was soon done, and food for all was prepared and enjoyed. It was a warm night, with a completely overcast sky, and soon after our usual evening prayers we white people were settled for the night. Light rain fell now and again and I pulled the big tarpaulin up over my swag.

Near by the aborigines lay alongside their little fires in the lee of windbreaks. The absolute quiet of the bush was broken only by the crying of the babies, to remind us that family life is the same the world over.

The camels, with ample food quite close to the camp, were looking at us in the morning instead of our looking for them. And what a beautiful scene the daylight brought us: the yellow, sharp sand of the creek, the red of the sandhill, the fresh green of the young buck-bush and the yellow of the Petermann wattles.

During the morning's ride Mt Curdie was visible soaring into the sky above the hills that shelter Lasseter's cave. We came back to the cave at lunch-time and on this occasion we dug two soaks for quicker filling of the canteens. Tjuintjara found a burrow from which he got two full-grown rabbits and four young ones. He gave them all to the women and children to cook on the fire, where native cucumbers were already being roasted. The aborigines had been getting plenty of yelka, the root bulbs of a coarse grass growing on the creek banks. These taste much like hazel nuts. We had noticed that during the fast travel of the previous day the men took turns in carrying the children, helping the womenfolk when they needed it. This gave the lie to the common belief that all burdens are always left to the women of the race.

One more night's camp and we were started on our final day's ride back to Piltardi, the base camp. During this day the natives again gathered many cucumbers, and the country was beautiful with wild flowers. We often came upon a particularly striking plant. Looked down on from the camels it appeared to be just a tuft of dull green grass, but all round the base of it close to the ground were bright red flowers. The plant was so prickly that we could never pull up a specimen, and we were in too great a hurry to unpack a shovel. The red part of the flower was a trumpet-shaped petal from which protruded ten bright yellow stamens. The sepals were very specialized, coming up from a cup and forming a hood over the trumpet. We learnt later the name of the plant was *Brachysema Chambersii*.

By lunchtime we had come to the Irvine River bed, and reached the Casterton in the late afternoon, when heavy rain was falling. One of the natives, standing on high ground, was waving his woomera as if trying to turn the rainstorm away from us to the hills. "Carpi," he called to me as he pointed to the rain falling some distance behind, and when I indicated what I thought he was trying to do he replied "Awa"—yes. When the rain reached us, men and women grabbed the youngest of the children and held them away from the storm. The natives looked very miserable in the rain and the wind.

As our camel team approached the base camp at Piltardi two of our aboriginal party from the Western Australian side, walking alongside the leading camels, stopped dead when they saw signs of a camp. Their alarm increased as they saw a white man walk towards us. But when we explained that all was well they came on.

By half past six we were dismounting, unpacking, and relieved that there would be no saddling and loading of camels in the morning. In our travelling along the Petermann Range we had seen no native game, and those of our party who had remained at Piltardi had seen only one euro, two wallabies, and several dingoes—clear evidence between us that the native food position in the Petermanns was very bad after the long drought. We turned in early and slept for ten hours. The trip had been strenuous, and for the first day back at the base camp there was hardly a word from anyone. During the afternoon we visited the folk who had travelled back with us. They were in a very happy mood. Tennis balls had no meaning for them until I threw one high in the air; then they outdid us in the height of their throws and laughed uproariously when the balls bounced high on landing.

On our ride back to Piltardi I had become very interested in the lad who had travelled apart from his people. Each evening soon after camping I had noticed that a particular girl of about twelve years was missing from the camp. Watching carefully from a distance one evening, I saw her go over to the lad some two hundred yards away. The boy was about sixteen years old, powerfully built, and had his hair gathered in a knot on the top of his head. He had not been through the first initiation rite—circumcision—which usually took place at the age of twelve or so. This was almost certainly due to the impossibility of getting enough men together at one place for the ceremony.

Corroborees can take place only where and when water and food are plentiful. These conditions had not been fulfilled during the past three years because of the prolonged drought, which forced small groups to travel far apart. I saw the girl sitting with the lad, sharing with him the edible roots, fruits, and vegetable food she had gathered during the day. It turned out that they were full brother and sister, the whole incident another example that in human qualities the aborigines are no different from ourselves.

Our first evening back at Piltardi—a Sunday—was one not to be forgotten. I remember the frightened faces of the tribal people when our wireless loud-speaker first operated in their presence. But our reassurance soon put them at ease, and one mother even brought her child up to the instrument. Later we all, dark and white alike, sat round for evening service. Mothers cuddled their tiny babies and little toddlers just as white mothers do, and every now and again a sleeping child would stretch an arm and relax just like one of our own. The services coming over the air from the cities of the South did not, we felt, fit the occasion, and so we switched off the wireless and held our own service with Pastor Albrecht speaking to the aborigines in their own tongue. We felt a sense of real fellowship with these fine primitive people and they were happy as they went off to lie down naked between their little fires of hot embers in the frosty night.

Next day I was cook and did all "kitchen" duties while the others saw to the trucks and re-arranged the stores. The tribal women were early astir, carrying water from the Piltardi waterhole and later the aboriginal camel-drivers, supplied with provisions for three weeks, left on their three hundred mile trip back to Hermannsburg with the camels. Our aboriginal friends were given payment for dog-scalps, and provided with a farewell meal. During the afternoon we visited their camp and made a note of their names. The children were smiling and friendly with us now, and showed no trace of the fear with which they first met us. One of the little girls had truly blonde hair, and two others were fair-haired. This golden hair, most attractive with the brown skin, is common in the Musgrave and Petermann aborigines, all people of the Pitjantjatjara tribe. Two of the girls and one of the mothers were very pretty, and another had a face of fine distinction. With soap and water, attention to hair, and pretty clothes these people could have taken their place anywhere. The men too were of a fine type. There was an old man, one old woman, and three babies. All but one of the women either had young babies or were pregnant—surely Nature's compensation for the recent loss of life in the tribe by drought.

That night as we settled to sleep, the camp looked very deserted without the camels and their drivers; we wondered how it would appear to the natives next day after we too had left with our trucks. For there seemed little likelihood that they would meet again with such a group as we were, unless the Federal Government opened a depot in the Range. But at that time, July 1939, neither the Governments nor the Christian Churches had faced their responsibility to the aboriginal people of Australia.

Next day breakfast was at sunrise and individually we paid the myalls a final visit when we were nearly ready to leave. For Tjuintjara there was a special farewell. As soon as we had reached Piltardi he had gone off to his wife and two sons, and had brought her to us with a very deep, infected burn on her ankle. This had called for very thorough treatment which she accepted trustfully. And now Tjuintjara was given an oil tin which had been completely cleansed and to which a handle had been fitted. He handed it to his wife; they spoke together and he very shyly thanked us. What a meagre reward it seemed for his unfailing guidance throughout the trip. But as a nomad he had no use for anything he could not carry and the gift was of real value to his wife.

It was a sad leave-taking. What would their future be? Would these people all starve in yet another drought? Would they drift into a cattle station or be moved on from place to place. We would never know. At 9 a.m. the trucks moved out; we were silent and the aborigines looked as sad as we felt.

All through the camel patrol the nights had been bitterly cold, nearly all below freezing point with the first night registering 20 deg. F. just after sunrise. I had never slept in so many clothes, and never been so cold on rising; I have a clear memory of those nights on the ground—the keen cutting wind that came just as dawn was about to break, and the absolute silence of the bush just before that. Then, with the first suspicion of the coming day, the birds broke out in song.

Certain incidents of this trip remained deeply printed in my memory: the two aboriginal men introducing themselves to us on the border of Western Australia; the little toddler wearing a necklet of bandicoot fur and sucking a sweet I gave her; the tall young man with the tall and pretty wife who didn't like any of us speaking to her for more than a minute or so; Pingeri, the blonde-haired little girl who shyly avoided me until I ignored her; the myall who took my box of matches and showed me how to light the fire in a strong wind with only one match; and two other incidents that showed real mother love and care. A baby I examined had severe bronchitis, and its upper air passages were blocked with phlegm. Whenever the child got to the stage of nearly choking the mother would suck the phlegm from the baby's nostrils and eject it vigorously. This may shock some people, but it must be remembered that these primitive folk were entirely on their own resources. The baby would have died but for its mother's action.

I was fortunate, too, in seeing something which gave the lie to the all too prevalent idea that aborigines are dirty in their habits. A mother held out her baby when its bowels moved, then very gently scraped the baby's skin with a thin flat stone and lightly dusted its buttocks with fine sand. The child was then put on its feet. Some years later a primitive mother was staying in our home with her baby, who was an out-patient at the Children's Hospital. My wife has often spoken of the unconcealed disgust of this bush mother when my wife tried to instuct her how to use napkins for the child and how best to wash them when they were soiled!

On the return truck journey from Piltardi to Ernabella we found the ground firm, and following our outward tracks we were soon back in the Musgrave Ranges where conditions were in great contrast to those we had found in the Petermanns. Vegetable food and game—kangaroos, euros, and emus—were in abundance and several wild turkeys were seen. The aboriginal people looked hale and hearty, and there were a large number of children. A few miles out of Ernabella, however, we came on a great many ill-conditioned myalls making for the Mission. With the exception of one Ernabella man they had all come from the Petermann country where we had been. They must have left there before we set out, and it is almost certain the Ernabella man made the trip to bring them in.

Although desperately tired on arrival at Ernabella, some of us by invitation went out that night to a near-by hillside to see a corroboree. It was the "work-up" to the circumcision of a novice from the Everard Range, sixty miles south of the Musgraves. There were forty men pounding the ground with sticks and chanting their songs. The novitiate, on the one occasion we saw him raised from the prone position and thrown up, looked the picture of misery. He was kept lying face down at full length, his head at the edge of a circle of men. There were two of these groups of men, each round a small fire. The lad's head was covered and one man had a knee on his shoulder while another had a knee on his hip. The ceremony continued far into the night and morning.

The following day I did a full day's inspection of the Mission sheep camps and came back very tired. Next morning was spent in examination and treatment of sick people; there was a bitter wind blowing, and a number of people had severe colds, one having pneumonia. Some children were suffering from discharging ears and burns were common, from their sleeping close to the small fires. I also found several cases of near-blindness in older people. About one hundred and sixty people were present in the camp, where the children were racing about happily.

After a restful Sunday I was packing up on Monday morning when a woman came running from the camp calling out in evident distress. She was thoroughly dazed, suffering from concussion and crying irrationally. Her scalp was split to the skull in two places, and there was a very large swelling on her elbow. Her husband, Lalili, was the aggressor. He had been severely taken to task by the Superintendent for spearing Mission goats and evidently thought that his wife had given him away. We shall hear again of Lalili.

At Mt Cavanagh cattle station on our way to the railway we met a white man well known in the district who had been collecting dog-scalps from the natives of the Mann and Tomkinson Ranges in the South Australian section of the Central Aborigines' Reserve. He described the aborigines there as "merely skin and bone," and said that many had died. The myall natives of the Petermanns had told us that it was west of the Mann Range that people had died after going south in the hope of finding better conditions.

Back at the Finke siding we found there had been much rain since we had arrived from the south five weeks ago. Vegetation had increased noticeably; there was water everywhere along the railway and at Lake Eyre water was within two hundred yards of the line—closer than I had ever seen it before. Creeks everywhere were "running a banker." At Port Augusta we bought a newspaper, our first for five weeks, and read a proposal that the State wheat acreage should be reduced!

We took this badly, having just returned from a drought-stricken Interior where human beings had died from lack of food.

The end of the year 1939 was marked by the passing of a new Aborigines Act for South Australia. This was in some ways an improvement on the Act it amended, but in one important respect it was regressive. Its definition of "aborigine" brought under the control of a Government Board every person of any aboriginal blood. No matter how well educated an aboriginal might be, no matter what his or her standing in the community, the status of full citizen was denied unless by special exemption from the Act.

Unconditional exemptions from the Act could be granted on the basis of "character, standard of intelligence, and development" (Section 11a) and when granted were irrevocable. The Board administering the Act could, however, if it thought fit, declare a limited exemption which it might revoke at any time during a period of three years if the person did not prove to be of "such character, standard of intelligence and development to justify the continuance of the declaration." If not revoked during the three-year period it automatically became unconditional and irrevocable.

In actual practice the Board has been hesitant to grant unconditional exemptions, and I know of one double-certificated trained nurse who received notification of "limited" exemption without her having made any application at all. One cannot help wondering how the rest of us would fare if our citizenship were based on "character, standard of intelligence, and development!"

71

It is not difficult to understand why so many part-aborigines have refused to apply for exemption, preferring to ignore the existence of the Act.

One of the Federal implications of this law, and similar Aborigines Acts in other States, has been that unless exempted, aborigines with more than fifty per cent aboriginal blood, even if paying income tax, were not able to claim Social Service benefits. Child endowment was an exception to this, and in certain circumstances sickness and unemployment benefits. In 1959 this discrimination was ended by the Federal Government, and all natives not nomadic or primitive became eligible for all social services, but in the words of the Minister for Social Services, the Hon. H. S. Robertson, "for more than fifty years social service benefits were not paid to aboriginal natives unless they were exempt from the State native welfare laws."

It was in this year also, June 1939, that a census of aborigines was taken, and the Commonwealth Statistician's report was released in Canberra on 1 February 1940. It showed for the first time an increase in the full-blood population with a substantial proportion of women and children indicating that the upward trend was likely to continue. Since 1901 half-caste aborigines had more than trebled in number.

By this time the 1939-45 war was in progress, and Sir Henry Gullett, the Minister for External Affairs, expressed regret that the Federal grant for aborigines had been reduced because of defence needs. "I am aware," he said, "of our appalling record in regard to aborigines and know of no greater indictment against Australia than the fate of the original owners of this country."

Not only was the grant reduced, but it was announced later in the year in Darwin, on 13 November, that the town's Aboriginal Compound was to be converted into a military hospital, and that three hundred aborigines would be homeless. That happened a week later.

In the winter of 1940 I visited South Australian aboriginal settlements on the River Murray and on the Nullarbor Plain. Small camps existed at different parts along the river, and the people were dependent on seasonal fruit-picking for a living. At other times rabbits and sometimes fish provided a meal. I called at one of these at Swan Reach, where the United Aborigines Mission had a Faith Mission on the edge of the river.

Forty adults and thirty-five children were living on a very restricted plot, all the valuable land having been taken up by a white man. His very fine house was alongside the Mission, providing a grim contrast to the Mission shacks, which were of hessian and set very close together. Several of these had cement floors and they were damp and cold. Diet was inadequate and medical attention spasmodic. Most of the medical care and all sick nursing was done by a married couple untrained in such work. Children were growing up in unhealthy surroundings, devoid of any wholesome diet, proper education, and training for life.

On the other side of the river was a small sandy area set aside for natives, a site quite unsuitable for permanent housing. Further up the river there was a larger native reserve, but very little of it was of any value for agriculture.

The following month I went to an entirely different part of the State—to Ooldea on the East-West railway line that crosses the Nullarbor Plain. Reports were that a large number of ill-clad, ill-fed aborigines frequented the railway line, selling curios to travellers and seeking scraps of meat at the fettlers' camps. There was some truth in these rumours, but at fettlers' camps some of the aboriginal men were paid for cutting firewood, and the money was spent at the mission store for extra food. Game to supplement rations provided by the Government did not exist anywhere near. The mission of four houses for white staff was set among sandhills, and there was a dormitory building of two overcrowded rooms housing eleven girls and nine boys. These children were regarded by the mission as a special charge, and in addition to the basic Government ration of flour, tea, and sugar they got meat, milk syrup, and jam from the mission, plus an extra Government ration of rice and peas.

The contrast between these twenty children and those on the basic ration was manifest—in build, in appearance, and in physical and mental activity—in fact the difference was startling. The twenty schoolchildren and another fifty from the camp had a hot bath on Saturdays, the water being changed after every twelve.

At the request of the missionary in charge I examined the dormitory children, all of whom were recovering from whooping cough. One baby in the camp was very ill with capillary bronchitis and was put on special treatment at once—it recovered.

The "running ear" was in evidence; in my experience present in every aboriginal camp. The very sick people were brought to the mission compound to be under supervision. There was one bright spot: one of the missionaries was a trained State School teacher, and the school work achieved was a credit to her and to the children in such primitive conditions. I was horrified when she told me she was to be taken for other duties and replaced by a totally untrained person.

Ooldea was a most unsuitable place for a ration depot or a mission. It was nothing but loose sand and sandhills, with stunted scrub in the distance. All the aborigines were full-bloods, some with corroboree headgear; but all wore clothing of a kind. The number seemed to vary between two hundred and three hundred, all leading a pauper existence. But food and clothing should not be given for nothing, even to tribal, or semi-tribal people; work should be made available at wages commensurate with work done. The fact was that no work could be started among the sandhills at Ooldea. This whole visit was completely depressing, but an event in the Northern Territory —the death of Lalili—was even more so.

7

Lalili And Others

LALILI, A FULL-BLOOD man whom I had known at Ernabella, was alleged to have been murdered in the Northern Territory just north of the border. His wife and relatives had fled to the Ernabella Mission in a state of abject grief. They told how Lalili had been attacked by a station owner and another white man, hit on the head with the butt of a pistol, tied to the back of a truck with fencing wire, and the truck driven to the homestead. It was utterly wrong that an immediate wireless report of the alleged murder was not made from the Mission. It was not until some weeks later when the Mission truck was at the Finke siding that the matter was reported to the police, and following inquiries the two men were arrested.

A Coroner's inquest was held in Alice Springs on 29th and 30th January 1941. Five aborigines gave evidence which according to the *Advertiser,* Adelaide, "in the main was in line with that of the arresting officer." Exhibits in court were a Luger pistol, a Lee-Enfield rifle, a piece of wire, and a human head. The Government medical officer was unable to discern any sign of injury on the head, and expressed an opinion that the head was more like that of a female than a male. The following day, in spite of this medical report on the supposed head of Lalili, the Coroner found that the two men had "murdered an aborigine called Lullilicki or Lollylegs on or about Dec. 14th, 1940."

The trial was held in the Supreme Court of the Northern Territory at Alice Springs on the 16th and 17th April 1941, in the absence of the arresting constable and of three of the witnesses. These three witnesses were said to have run away, but it was the invariable custom in the Northern Territory for aboriginal witnesses to be kept in strict custody until a trial was over. The barrister who was counsel for defence made the obvious point that the evidence was not such as to prove that the head produced was that of Lullilicki; the jury brought in a verdict of not guilty. I knew this powerfully built "Lullilicki," and had his photograph showing his long dark beard; there could be no possibility of mistaking the head of a female for his. One might have supposed that, in view of the opinion of the Government medical officer, an enquiry would have been made as to the possible death of a female aboriginal at about the same time at the alleged murder of Lullilicki and at about the same place. No such enquiry was made.

Although the two men were acquitted of murder they had during the trial admitted conduct of such cruelty as to result in the withdrawal from the station-owner of the Federal Government's permission to employ natives.

They had gone to the camp of "Lollylegs," as he was called in Court, on the day in question, searched his ration bags and concluded they contained rations that Lollylegs had no right to possess; they had an altercation with Lollylegs but as both men were armed had been able to overpower him. They then procured a length of wire about sixteen feet long, doubled it, fastened one end round his neck and then attached the loose end of this doubled wire to the back of the truck, and drove it to the homestead about six hundred yards distant; the truck which had a four-gear transmission box was driven in third gear. In the opinion of the two accused their action was justified by the need to be "firm with aborigines" on the property.

In conclusion I must quote from a letter written by the secretary of the Aborigines' Protection League, South Australia, of which I was President, to the Minister for the Interior, Canberra. The letter is dated 18 February, 1941, after the Coroner's inquest and two months before the trial. My purpose in quoting this letter is to show how determined were the efforts made to find out the truth of the whole matter at the time.

> This League is astonished that the whole corpus of the dead man was not taken to Alice Springs for the Coroner's inquest. . . . Only the head was taken and Dr — is reported as expressing an opinion that the skull was more like that of a female. When Constable — exhumed the body it had been buried so recently that there should have been no difficulty in telling whether the skull was that of a male or female. The

doubt has naturally arisen as to whether a wrong head was taken to the inquest. In view of the fact that the whole corpus was not on view at the Coroner's inquest on January 29th, 1941, this League begs that the body from which the head was taken be viewed at once while there is yet time to decide on the sex of the decapitated body. As the inquest on Jan. 29th was apparently held only on the head and not *super visum corporis* this League submits there is jurisdiction for its request above stated.

The following answer was received dated 25 February, 1941:

Dear Sir,

I am in receipt of your letter concerning the death of the native Lalili or Lullilicki at — Station near — and I am having inquiries made into the matter.

I shall communicate with you again on this subject immediately I am in a position to do so.

Yours sincerely,
H. S. Foll.

Presumably the Minister was never "in a position to do so," as no further letter was received. Nor has Lullilicki ever been seen or heard of since.

Another investigation in 1942 resulted in the cancelling of a man's licence to employ aborigines, the licence, by the way, costing only ten shillings and not specifying conditions of employment.

Constable V. C. Hall of the Northern Territory police force, found appalling conditions at a mining camp. No wages were being paid to the aboriginal workers, their food was very inadequate, and no food of any kind was being provided for the dependants, who were in a desperate state. Constable Hall was adjudged by his superior officer to have been too impetuous in cancelling the licence! He resigned.

Reference has already been made to the immediate effect of the outbreak of war on aboriginal policy—the reduction of Federal grant for aborigines announced by Sir Henry Gullett. During the years of Australia's war effort little was heard in the south about full-blood aborigines, but they were much in evidence in the Northern Territory. The men were formed into a labour force at the low wage of tenpence a day, and poor diet for the work done. This matter is dealt with fully in my chapter "Sustenance . . . Disease . . . Shelter."

Some natives, however, in the Territory benefited greatly by the attention of Army medical officers who, in their spare time, travelled in mobile medical units among bush aborigines. Sores on the body disappeared, and infections of the eye cleared up. Another interesting result of the war situation was the evacuation of half-caste children from institutions and missions in the danger area when the Japanese raids on Darwin began. These children were taken to the south, where they attended the ordinary State schools and proved that in mental and physical prowess they were not inferior to white children. The Federal Government had guaranteed their return when it became safe, but some of them found work and a permanent place in the community life of the south.

As the war drew to a close many cases of cruelty to aborigines came to light. In 1944 a station-owner in South Australia complained to a policeman that the wild-dog fence of his property had been damaged. The policeman found some aborigines who had gone through the fence for water. He burned their wurlies, hunting spears, and blankets, then took the women's billycans and made a hole in the bottom of each. This, too, in hot weather.

The following year a cattle owner with a policeman and black-tracker, all armed, rounded up natives on his property and put four men in chains. Other aborigines were forced to pile up blankets and food-gathering equipment—spears, woomeras, and pitis—in a heap. All their dogs except two were shot, and the people were then driven off with violence. One man was so severely beaten that he could not get up, and his wife carried him pick-a-back for twelve miles to a well. Another man had to be left where he fell; another badly hurt was a highly respected old man.

All the aborigines treated in this wanton, ruthless fashion were decent, inoffensive tribal people living in their own country. The station-owner and the policeman had conveniently forgotten that although cattle had been introduced, it was provided for by law that the aborigines have access to water and game. When questioned afterwards the station-owner admitted that the natives were not doing any harm.

In the same year the owner of an isolated cattle station was tried for the flogging of an aboriginal tied to a tree. It was stated in the Supreme Court at Alice Springs that four waddies four feet in length were used; as one broke another was taken from the pile. The report of the patrol officer of the Native Affairs Department was completely corroborated by a half-caste stockman, who, said the *News,* Adelaide of 3 August, 1945, gave evidence that he had assisted the station owner to tie the aboriginal to the tree.

But a white jury found the accused not guilty.

In December, however, another station-owner was actually found guilty of assault and fined one hundred and thirty-five pounds plus costs. *The Advertiser,* Adelaide, reported that the charges were that he had assaulted M. by chaining him by the neck to a tree and striking him with fists and a revolver; assaulted F. and W. by chaining them by their necks to a fence; assaulted J. J. and J. by chaining them to a dray. When the manager was found guilty several station people declared that they regarded the verdict as a challenge to their "control" of natives. Such an attitude explains a statement made by the Minister for the Interior, Mr Johnson, on his return at this time from a trip to the back country and reported in the *Sun News Pictorial* of 12 November, 1945:

"In many cases cattle stations are using black labour under almost slave conditions."

Next winter during school holidays my wife and I and family, two of our own and a full-blood aboriginal boy, set off by train from Adelaide to Finke in the Northern Territory *en route* for the Ernabella Mission. At breakfast, our first meal on the Commonwealth railway, we decided that if exception were taken to the aboriginal boy having meals with us in the dining car we would leave the train. The steward, after asking my wife what she, Andrew, and Rosemary would have, said "What will he have?" The smiling little aboriginal boy immediately replied "I'll have porridge thank you, with eggs and bacon to follow." I thought the waiter was going to lose his balance! We didn't have to leave the train.

We reached Finke while it was still dark and the children were still in bed. Hurriedly we dressed and were relieved to see one of the missionaries, Mr R. Henderson, waiting for us at the line with his lantern. Cases and sleeping swags were handed down to him and we left the train, only to discover that our carefully packed food supply was not on that train at all, but would arrive by a goods train at noon. My wife was somewhat dismayed, as she rather feared for the condition of the pounds of butter she had packed, a real luxury on the mission in those early days.

We were well cared for, however, and after a much-appreciated cup of tea with the storekeeper and his wife we enjoyed a breakfast cooked in the open. By half-past one the goods train had arrived, and soon afterwards we were safely away in the Ernabella truck. We drove till late afternoon, when we stopped for a meal and Mr Henderson rigged up the patrol wireless so that he could send news of our progress to the mission. At nine o'clock we made camp, setting out our swags in a sandy creek bed.

It was a memorable experience to sleep with one's family under the myriad of stars of that clear Central Australian sky. But in the early hours of the morning our peace was rudely interrupted by the alarming sound of cattle tramping through the creek where we lay. Half a dozen bulls churned up the sand between us and the little native fire by which one of our Ernabella men was sleeping!

We slept again, but were up early, and after breakfasting were soon on our way. It was fine to see the children deeply interested in everything, this being their first experience of Australia's real "outback." On the way we saw four different pairs of magnificent wedge-tailed eagles, five emus, and a great many kangaroos, one of which the driver shot and loaded on the truck.

For our picnic lunch my son, at that time a keen scout, contributed an excellent damper in which he had mixed a generous handful of currants and raisins. But in the hot midday sunshine the presence of myriads of flies made eating somewhat hazardous, and his mother and young sister regarded his damper with some suspicion!

A few hours' more driving brought us two miles or so from Ernabella, and here we were met by some of the mission natives whose keen hearing had picked up the approach of the truck long before it could be seen. As evening fell, and the truck pulled up out of the Ernabella creek bed, there was a great shout of

Girl sharing food with her uninitiated brother.

"Old Folk's Home" 1934, Alice Springs.

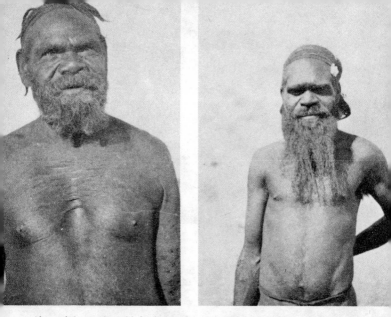

Above left — An old bushman from the Pitjantjatjara tribe, Musgrave Ranges. *Above right* — Tribal nomad, Musgrave Ranges. The belt round the waist and the binding on the head are made of human hair. White "flower" is a decoration made by whittling wood.

Above left — Tribal nomad, Musgrave Ranges. Scar on left arm due to yaws after treatment. *Above right* — Pitjantjatjara nomad.

welcome from the natives. We were soon at the residence of the Superintendent and his wife, The Rev and Mrs G. Wright, who gave us a warm welcome. Among the aboriginal people we looked especially for a lass who had stayed in our home three years before and had formed a strong friendship with our little daughter. I saw her face in the crowd, and when I called her by name, Nganyintja, she ran forward to greet us and to give Rosemary an especially affectionate welcome. After the four-day journey from Adelaide we were very appreciative of the hot baths that followed and we were soon asleep in comfortable beds, so comfortable that we were all late for breakfast next morning.

Life was strenuous at the mission in those early days, for there was much to be done. The Superintendent and his wife rose at five o'clock, breakfast was at seven for the mission staff and at eight for the native people. At nine o'clock the main work of the mission began—older girls went off to the various staff homes to learn something of our way of life; men went to muster horses or bring in firewood from surrounding country; goatherds led the goats off after milking, and other men worked in the vegetable garden.

For us perhaps the most interesting sight was the gathering of the children for school. In those first years of the mission no clothes were worn by the children and they arrived at the little schoolhouse dusty with red sand and the ashes of the small fires which kept them warm at night. They had great fun hosing each other down, and it was a merry sight to see the little gleaming bodies running about in the sunshine until they were warm and dry. Then came some formal schooling inside the building; the lessons were given in Pitjantjatjara, and no child attended against his will. No doubt this fact accounted for the very happy atmosphere of the school, and perhaps too for the noticeably keen concentration of the children.

Children would sometimes be absent from school for weeks at a time while out bush with their parents and would slip back into school quite naturally on their return. The teacher, South Australian Government-trained, told of her amazement at their retention of what they had learnt and of their little need for revision. The children sang for us, and we were much impressed with their ear for harmony; they sang in several parts, and at the teacher's direction changed parts with complete ease.

Later Nganyintja, who with one of her friends was assisting in the school, tried to teach our children one of their traditional aboriginal melodies. Andrew was anxious to master it in order to use it in his scout troop. But the attempt had to be abandoned—with much kindly laughter from the aboriginal girls at the white children's inability to pick up their musical scale.

I spent some time each day at the dispensary, a small, well-equipped room in charge of a trained and experienced nurse, Sister M. Turner. Sister was one of the busiest people on the staff, and attendances at the clinic were strong evidence of the faith the native people had in the white man's medicine. On one occasion I dressed a very severe burn on a baby boy who had rolled too close to the camp fire. In my city surgery I had never seen better handling by the mother of a child who was in great pain.

One evening as we sat at our meal with the Superintendent and his wife there was a knock at the door and several aboriginal girls were there with an invitation for Rosemary to go with them to a corroboree. It was made clear that the invitation did not include any other members of the family, but we knew she would be quite safe and happy with Nganyintja. After she had been away for two hours or more we began to wish the child were back. I walked a little way up a small hillside and not hearing any sound, I flashed my torch. An immediate response came from the youngsters, who broke into a haunting tribal air to let us know they were on the way.

My daughter told us afterwards of the welcome she had been given, and of how the other girls drew her head with theirs under covering so that she would not observe parts of the corroboree forbidden to women and girls. We felt that she had been especially honoured and accepted as a tribal sister to Nganyintja, and all through our visit she seemed to evoke special attention.

A few evenings later we were all invited to a song and dance round the camp fire, an entertainment in which both men and women joined. Once or twice I imitated the steps, and my efforts were greeted with uproarious laughter. It was a happy occasion for everyone.

One day the schoolchildren were given a special holiday on account of our visit and we went for a picnic with them. After a walk of three miles through the bush, during which the native children collected and shared a variety of vegetable foodstuffs, we reached a beautiful place in a dried creek bed with gum trees on the banks. The aboriginal children soon had holes dug in the sand and filled the billycans with the clean water that welled up. Fires were made, and we all enjoyed a hearty meal. Later games were played, and as the sun was warm our own children were really envious of the naked state of their playmates. As the afternoon wore on we started the long walk home, and found it necessary to carry some of the little ones as we neared Ernabella.

The games the tribal boys played were interesting to watch; most of the boys had light spears about five feet long and they practised the skill of accurate throwing. One lad with an underarm throw sent a circular piece of bark about six inches in diameter at speed along the ground. Each of the other boys threw a spear at it and there were frequent hits. This was practice for the days when they would be hunting animals for food. But there was a more serious form of play—training for the time when they might have to take part in fighting. Then the boys threw spears at one another; the throwing was accurate, and the boy aimed at needed to be alert and quick to dodge the spear with a deft movement of body or leg. One of the boys had a knee speared; it swelled up, and he was under my care for several days.

Several young men in their late teens were in the process of initiation into tribal manhood. During this period they were not allowed to be seen by the tribe, and camped at some distance from the mission. When visiting them I recognized schoolboys of earlier days, but missed one who had been very brilliant at arithmetic. He was, the others said, far out in the bush. During this time of separation from the tribe the "Nyinkas," as they were called, had to be completely responsible for their own subsistence.

Our last afternoon was spent in joining in a unique sports day. There were the usual flat races for boys and girls and young women. It was amusing as well as significant to see that the leaders in a race tended to wait until the slower runners came alongside, thus proving surely that co-operative achievement, not competitive striving, was their normal way of life. An interesting test of steady balance was the carrying of a billy of water on the head. One young woman ran at speed without spilling a drop!

Spear throwing at targets called for strength and accuracy—the longest throw being little short of ninety feet. But most fascinating to watch was the final contest—firemaking. A small dry branch was split, and the split filled with powdered tinder. Two little heaps of dry grass were laid ready on the ground alongside the branch, each end of which was held steady by a foot of a boy standing on it. Then the fire-maker squatting by the branch rapidly worked the hard edge of his woomera back and forward across the branch. Very soon smoke appeared, and the smoking tinder from the split branch was poured carefully on to one of the little heaps of grass and the other heap was carefully laid on top. Gentle waving of grass held in the hand and gentle blowing soon brought the flame.

When the excitement of the firemaking had died down, I produced a skipping-rope, and my demonstration caused great merriment. But my efforts were soon eclipsed by a younger man, Walter MacDougall, the sheep supervisor of the Mission. Then the aborigines took over and for some time there were shrieks of laughter from everyone. A special tea brought the happy afternoon to a close, and long after the people had returned to their wiltjas we heard their laughter.

Next day we set off by truck for our homeward journey. Nganyintja came with us on the trip to the Finke, and she and Rosemary spent two final happy days together. It was a sad little parting as the train drew out from the siding and we left our friends behind.

8

Measles The Killer

ONE OF AUSTRALIA'S outstanding journalists, Douglas Lockwood —a winner of several major literary awards—wrote a startling article from Darwin in December 1946. He described shocking examples of "callous, brutal and inhuman treatment" quoted by the Secretary of the Northern Australian Workers Union, Mr J. Walker. These reports had come from union members who had been droving in the Wave Hill and Victoria River Downs districts. The printed details of his article are too inhuman to reproduce, cruel and degrading beyond belief. They can be read in *The News* Adelaide, of 3 December 1946. And in the following day's issue of the same paper Douglas Lockwood continued the story, quoting a member of the executive of the Union, Mr Jack Meaney, who had been a cattle drover and stockman in the Territory stations for twenty years.

He was appalled by some of the instances of maltreatment he had seen, but he regarded the slow starvation of the people too old or sick to work as the worst feature. "Nothing," he said, "can justify the mass starvation and mass cruelty which is going on in the outback country. The Government is subsidising the pastoral industry with human lives." *The News'* leading article of that same day said:

> They [the allegations] presented such a harrowing picture—unfortunately not an unfamiliar one—that all fair-minded Australians will be definite that Mr Walker's charges should be officially and thoroughly investigated. That is the least that should be done. But because of the deal which has been given to natives over the years doubts arise whether the investigation will be made. The outlook where the well-being of natives is concerned is rarely promising.

That same day *The News* interviewed me and I stated that inhuman treatment of aborigines by whites in isolated places had always taken place and still went on. There were exceptions, but the general attitude of the white people in the Territory was that the native did not matter except as cheap labour.

The British film director Harry Watt was at that time in Adelaide, and he said he had been shocked at the way aboriginal workers were treated in the Northern Territory. He referred to them as "commercially exploited" and "suffering under laws that were distinctly colonial." He cited the following case.

> The Overlanders was on location two hundred miles from Alice Springs. It was a cold day, and the aboriginal —a particularly good worker whom we all liked—took shelter in the cabin of a white man's truck. When the white man turned up he abused the native for daring to sit inside and turned him out. Later the aboriginal remarked to an Australian Army driver that he'd have liked to have "donged" the white man. Apparently the driver talked, for a policeman came two hundred miles from Alice Springs and arrested the aboriginal on a charge of having "uttered a threat against a white man."

The prisoner was taken to Alice Springs but after a strong protest by the film unit he was freed and was back within twenty-four hours.

Mr Watt said that his unit was criticized in the Northern Territory for "spoiling" the aboriginal workers. They were paid full award rates, given adequate meals, and where possible provided with proper bedding and beds. Even the local authorities charged with protecting the aborigines objected because the men were paid in full. "Apparently we should have paid the aboriginal workers something like £1 a week and given the remainder to the Government Department controlling them."

"In Alice Springs," said Mr Watt, "I met a man who said he had made £42,000 admittedly with the help of aboriginal labour, yet housed his workers in shocking bag humpies and provided indescribably poor living conditions."

I have given in full this interview from *The News* Adelaide, 7 December 1946, as it gives a clear picture of impressions gained by a visitor to Australia's outback.

An appeal was made at this time to the United Nations on behalf of natives of the North-West of Western Australia. This appeal resulted from a strike which had taken place in the previous May; eight hundred station hands had struck for a minimum wage of thirty shillings a week, and a number of them had been arrested.

Soon afterwards, in February 1947, a hundred full-blood aborigines employed as domestics and general helps in Darwin homes and Government Departments went on strike. Domestics in private homes were generally receiving ten shillings a week, but some only five shillings. Government Departments paid men thirty shillings a week, of which ten shillings was paid direct to the worker and one pound went into a trust fund. Within ten days of the strike the Government decided to pay its native workers thirty shillings a week in cash, and to provide clothing, food, and housing.

At this time a conference was being held in Alice Springs between the Department of Native Affairs and pastoralists employing aborigines. No representatives of employees or of trade unions were allowed to attend, and the Press was excluded. A scale of wages was agreed to, some of the items being:

> The wage per week for an experienced adult male employee will be £1 placed to his credit plus his rations and tobacco and plus the entire upkeep by the station of one wife and one child. Males who have completed less than three years service will be paid 12/6 a week in the first year, 15/- in the second year and 17/6 in the third. A female who is married to an employee and working will get 7/6 per week and keep, but if unmarried or not the maintained wife of an employee will get 10/- and keep while working. Stations will not be responsible for the maintenance of any aborigines but may agree to provide rations and clothing for them, the cost to be borne by the administration. Clothing and tobacco will be sold to employees at net landed station cost. Aborigines while employed as drovers with cattle will be paid 15/- per week in addition to the prescribed rate.

Though excluded from the actual conference the Press received a statement from which the following is an excerpt.

This Conference was decided upon with the view to attempting to establish an improved standard of employment in the pastoral industry in the Northern Territory. The Conference was historic inasmuch as it is the first of its kind ever held, *and taking into......* *consideration the fact that in the past as a general rule no actual cash payment has been made to the employee this decision must be regarded as satisfactory!!!*

The next Conference of importance was one held in 1948 at Canberra when a programme for aborigines' welfare was agreed upon by native welfare officials of the Northern Territory and the States. But Mr Johnson, then Minister for the Interior, after touring the Northern Territory and interviewing local residents, station-owners, and police said that he was not happy with much that he had seen. "My complaint is," he said, "that in the Northern Territory this programme has not been given effect to." In the same month that the Minister made this statement (21 April 1949) there was strong confirmation of his complaint in an article in the Darwin *Standard*. George Gibbs told of conditions on "Wave Hill station owned by Vesteys" where nearly two hundred and fifty aborigines were employed. "No wages were paid to any native—food issue includes a slice of bread and a hunk of beef per meal—tea is made and there is a fair issue of sugar." The Company profits were tax free. There were thirty-three aboriginal children under seven years and thirty-seven under ten years on the Station entirely without education. Few if any stations provided adequate shelter for sleeping, washing, and feeding for their aboriginal families. The aborigines did the hard work, but their food was vastly inferior to that of the white man, and the sub-nutrition resulted in lowered resistance to disease.

Government ordinances regulating wages, food, and accommodation were often dead letters. How far this was so was maintained by G. R. Birt of Adelaide in the *Advertiser* of 6 April 1950.

Recently I visited the Northern Territory after seven years of absence and I particularly observed the conditions of the natives. In the Victoria River district [Victoria River cattle station is the largest in Australia] where I was stationed as a police officer just over 15 years ago, I noted a marked diminution in the aboriginal population, so much so that pastoralists are complaining about a shortage of native labour. In my opinion the station owners are largely responsible for this, as the staple diet for native employees still appears to be bread and beef and not much of that. Lacking nourishing food containing the necessary vitamins it is not surprising that aborigines submit to illness easily. And yet I heard them reviled as "niggers," "coons," "lazy swine," etc., when sometimes they were unable to do the quantity of work expected of them. It was ironical that on one cattle station where semi-slavery conditions are particularly noticeable, Sunday School is held regularly for white children only.

Soon afterwards the Minister for the Interior of the newly elected Federal Government, The Hon P. A. McBride, after a two-week tour of the Northern Territory said:

> From the little I have seen and from information coming before me I am satisfied that there is much room for improvement in the administration of native affairs.

Thus within the same year the Ministers for the Interior in two administrations, Labour and Liberal, had admitted the unsatisfactory treatment of aborigines in the Northern Territory. Following this the whole matter of national responsibility for the aborigines was strongly emphasized by a private member, Mr Paul Hasluck, who said:

> The Commonwealth Parliament as the supreme voice of the Australian nation to ensure that, irrespective of where constitutional powers lie, the practical task of the betterment of the conditions of the natives throughout the Commonwealth shall be undertaken.

He reminded Parliament that already two Conferences of Commonwealth and State representatives to discuss native affairs had taken place at Canberra, in 1937 and 1948, but "action that followed bore little relation to the extensiveness of the recommendations."

"Now," he said, "we should consider starting a new era in which positive and effective action is likely to be taken."

In 1951 Mr Hasluck was appointed Minister for Territories —a new portfolio—and as such he was made responsible for the welfare of aborigines in the Northern Territory as well as for the natives of Papua and New Guinea. His appointment has resulted in a decade of gradual advancement for aborigines under his care, and this needs only to be matched by the complete social acceptance which he constantly advocates.

The early months of 1948 saw a devastating epidemic of measles in the centre of Australia, brought into Alice Springs unwittingly by a white child returning from school in the south. It swept through the native people in the Northern Territory and in northern South Australia.

The Commonwealth Health Medical Officer and Flying Doctor at Alice Springs was Dr W. Alderman. He was the only medical practitioner in a hundred thousand square miles and he did yeoman service throughout the epidemic in his vast area. In April it was reported by radio telegram that the epidemic, complicated by broncho-pneumonia, was raging at the Ernabella Mission, and the Aborigines Protection Board of South Australia flew me to Oodnadatta. From there a neighbour's truck took me the further three hundred miles to Ernabella.

Arriving at the mission late in the afternoon I found a state of complete emergency. Instead of getting a glad welcome as usual from some sixty aboriginal children and many of their parents we drove in with only an odd native about. All about the homestead and the hospital dispensary was the unusual sight of campfires, and lying on the ground behind hastily erected windbreaks were some three hundred aborigines, quite a number having been brought in from neighbouring stations.

Dr Alderman got in touch with me by wireless immediately on my arrival at the mission, and I was able to assure him that the Commonwealth Health Department and the Aborigines Protection Board in Adelaide had provided me with ample supplies of sulphadiazine, penicillin, and invalid foods. But the death rate was high; the staff of six were tired out—they had been on duty eighteen hours a day for nearly three weeks, and there was only one trained nurse. I sent a wireless message to the Aborigines Department asking for a general helper and for another trained nurse. A young woman who was holidaying in Alice Springs flew in, and a Sister was sent from Adelaide by air.

Night workers—and everyone was rostered for a share in it —had a very anxious time. Many of the patients were too sick to worry about keeping their little fires burning, and some of the delirious ones started walking away naked in the night. Had they got right away they would have died, for the nights were very cold. They had to be brought back at once and settled down again by their fires.

In the early stages of the epidemic Sister found some reluctance in the people to take the treatment, but after a few days those receiving it were so much better that all were anxious to have it. There were two incidents with native medicine men. They went into the little four-bed hospital and started pummelling the very sick ones to drive out the devil of sickness. But Sister's treatment proved itself and the incidents ceased.

Feeding was as important as drugs. The sick had to be given special food, and the worst cases had to be coaxed and hand-fed every two or three hours. The strain on the small staff was intense as there was not one aboriginal fit to help with wood cutting, washing, or making of bread. The Superintendent himself was cooking all the food for the natives and taking it round three times a day. Perhaps the hardest-worked man was the sheep overseer. For a time nearly all his shepherds were sick, and he had to visit the scattered sheep camps daily instead of the usual once a week.

By the time I left for home the situation at Ernabella was under control, but the epidemic was spreading westwards from the railway line through the Centre. Probably never before had the station people realized how much they needed aborigines in their work. I had treated cases at Oodnadatta, on the track, and at cattle stations, as well as at the Mission. There were many deaths at cattle stations and in the bush. To combat any future epidemic of measles among tribal aborigines I recommended gamma globulin pooled human serum be provided free by the Commonwealth Government. In Malaya the Government in this way reduced native deaths to a minimum.

While I was at Oodnadatta I had inspected the housing of aborigines working in the townships. It was no better than when I had seen it in 1935. The hovels still consisted of three-feet high humpies made of petrol drums, scrap iron, and bags. On both occasions I reported the matter to the South Australian Aborigines Department but no action was taken.

In 1949 I revisited Ernabella Mission and was warmly welcomed by the people. In a review of the epidemic of the year before, I found that not one of the aborigines who had been through the school nor one of the pupils had died of measles or its complications. The extra feeding at school had surely made the difference.

By 1949 forty to fifty children were in daily attendance at the new school building, and the trained teacher in charge had a progress report of every pupil. Teaching was still given in the aboriginal tongue and the teacher was ably supported by three young aboriginal women who had been through the school. The free expression pastel work and painting of the children were remarkably fine, and they showed a gift for a unique type of design which was historically valuable. They excelled, too, in part-singing, which even the very young children seemed to find natural and easy.

Craft work also was developing. In a dry creek bed the older women were spinning sheep's wool with the primitive spinning stick which has spun human hair for use and ornament for thousands of years. In the near-by craft-room the younger women were working looms and performing other techniques. Rugs, baby blankets, and hand-painted silk scarves were among the articles produced. Very beautiful hand-painted Christmas cards were being done by some of the senior girls using their own peculiar designs.

A new feature was a weekly afternoon devotional gathering for the women led by women of the mission staff. This was followed by a half an hour's folk dancing which the younger women especially enjoyed. Another development in the year since my last visit was the completion of the air-strip, the primary purpose of which was to accommodate the Flying Doctor.

One day I noticed that the native people had moved their camp to the shelter of a high bank, and I wondered why. Next morning I knew. During the night the barometer fell rapidly, and there was a fierce windstorm. Morning showed their former camp site swept clear of everything. The aborigines have an uncanny sense of impending weather change.

I was invited to attend an evening corroboree at the close of which five boys went through the first initiation ceremony. On another occasion I accompanied the staff and young native people to a picnic eighteen miles out alongside a large clay-pan covered with shallow water. The children rushed on to the clay-pan, and soon they were scattered over the wide expanse doing exactly as children in Scotland do on ice—sliding on the slippery surface. Now and again one of the younger children fell over, but in the absence of clothes that presented no problem!

Later that day our interest was aroused by some chanting and rhythmic beating of sticks on the ground. On investigating we found a boys' corroboree was being enacted. They carried on with complete concentration, not taking the slightest notice of us when we arrived on the scene. Here were naked myall children copying their fathers just as our own children do.

A young woman from Glasgow was visiting Ernabella at this time, and one evening she joined the aboriginal girls in their camp and spent the night with them. On joining us in the morning she was thoroughly excited about what she had seen the evening before. A girl in her teens, Nganyintja, of whom we have already heard, had performed the emu dance. "It was perfect," she said; "one of the finest bits of portrayal and mimicry I have ever seen."

9

Darwin To Adelaide

MY PLAN TO visit Darwin in 1934 had been interrupted by events at Alice Springs described in an earlier chapter. It was not till July 1951 that I was able to make the trip. Mr Hasluck, by then Minister for Territories, gave me every facility to visit Government settlements and reserves in and around Darwin. I also visited the native ward at the Public Hospital, the Leprosarium at Channel Island, and missions on islands along the coast and in Arnhem Land. I had interviews with the President and Secretary of the Half-Caste Progressive Association, the editor of the *Northern Standard,* and the organizer of the Northern Australian Workers' Union.

Bagot Reserve on the outskirts of Darwin is a compound for full-bloods. The men were taken to and from work in a huge iron-mesh cage-truck which was grossly overcrowded, and although some seats were provided nearly everyone stood. Men in Darwin were being paid two pounds a week, but there were no women in Government employment. At Bagot there was free housing, food, and clothing; and the Compound had a school and a hospital. The school was being very efficiently run by a keen headmaster under the new Commonwealth Education scheme for full-bloods, which was in its infancy.

I was pleased to see that children who were suffering from the early non-infectious stage of Hansen's disease being treated in the general Bagot hospital and not being sent to the Leprosarium. This enlightened policy had already led to some children actually being brought in by their parents for treatment. Dr Watsford, newly appointed Director of Health in Darwin, was also sending leprosy drugs to the missions for use on the spot.

Next door to Bagot Reserve was a home for part-aboriginal children, owned by the Aborigines Inland Mission, an undenominational body caring for aborigines in different parts of Australia. There were forty-four girls and thirty-seven boys in the home, those of school age being taken in an ordinary bus to and from the public school in Darwin. The contrast in method of transport of full-bloods of the Compound and the half-castes of the Home was glaring.

Delissaville Reserve, near Darwin, was reached by motor launch across the Harbour and through the mangroves, and was a one and a half hour run. Delissaville housed aborigines who had come from the Daly River area south and west of Darwin, but it was also used as a disciplinary centre, mostly for liquor offences.

Parap, a suburb of Darwin, had for housing large, airy, steel-framed army huts left over from the war, in which white and part-white people were living. At "Police Paddock" near Parap only half-castes lived, but here the huts, whose framework was of wood, were in serious disrepair from the ravages of white ants. Berrimah Reserve, close to Darwin, was scrub country held for aborigines from Arnhem Land. With one or two exceptions, the huts here had rotted away.

At the Department of Health I conferred with Dr Watsford, who was engaged in making a double-indexed card record of aborigines of the Territory and their ailments. Leprosy, tuberculosis, hookworm disease, and yaws were all prevalent. After my talk with Dr Watsford, Dr Alderman accompanied me to the Darwin Hospital where I visited the native wards. Here I found everything excellently done. Dr Alderman knew every patient by name, and there was clearly no difference in the treatment of whites and aborigines.

In the afternoon I was driven to the wharf where the mission luggers were loading. It was a beautiful sight. Many small craft painted white were riding at anchor on the shore side of the wharf; a steamer from Western Australia was unloading on the other side; and the wharf was crowded with lorries. One Methodist Mission lugger was manned entirely by native crew; the other had a white captain with crew of five aborigines.

I spent an afternoon at Channel Island with the aborigines suffering from leprosy. They were being treated and cared for with great devotion by Sisters of Our Lady of the Sacred Heart, assisted by a Brother.

With the Rev Ern Clark, a man of many years service in the Pacific Islands, I sailed from Darwin for Croker Island on the *Arietta,* an aboriginal-manned lugger with a young white missionary in charge. The weather was rough, causing us at times to shelter in the lee of headlands. On the floor of the cabin were two very young half-caste children, a boy and a girl, seasick as I was when I got down to help them.

At Cape Don lighthouse two aborigines paddled out in a dug-out canoe. We took a woman and three children on board and the men followed in the canoe, towed behind. Croker Island had its full-blood inhabitants but the great majority of the people we met were half-caste children brought from the mainland by the Government to be trained at a Methodist mission on the island. On reaching the age of eighteen the young people were free to return to Darwin. The island covered about a hundred and twenty square miles, and was two or three miles from the mainland, where the mission had timber rights and the right to shoot buffaloes. While I was at Croker there happened to be a party of aborigines buffalo shooting on the mainland, and they had an arrangement with their friends that each Friday afternoon they would send up a smoke signal if all was well with them. As the smoke rose in the air across the water, we experienced a very warm human feeling.

Life on the island was full of interest; cypress pine from the mainland was brought over to be cut at the sawmill; beef-cattle were being raised; beautiful brooches were made from sea-shells; and the island boasted an excellent fruit and vegetable garden. I partciularly enjoyed the fishing, trevalli and large pike being plentiful. Whereas we used hook and line, the natives still preferred the spear, and they got a dugong.

The schoolchildren here were a particularly happy lot. They were housed in cottage dormitories presided over by members of staff and senior pupils. Some of these seniors were youngsters who had returned after evacuation to New South Wales in the war years. While attending local State schools they had acquitted themselves well, some of them gaining public examination certificates.

One day I was interested to watch the arrival of a plane at the mission. It was a small Commonwealth Medical Service plane, and the pilot was accompanied by a nursing sister. Behind them was sitting an Elcho Island aboriginal returning from Darwin hospital. The plane touched down at Croker bringing home a six-month-old baby. The baby had been born with a harelip and a cleft palate; the deformed lip had been

An Ernabella schoolgirl

The golden hair of the Pitjantjatjara full-bloods.

corrected at Darwin hospital, and the palate would be operated on later. After Sister had handed over the baby to Mrs Johncock, wife of the Superintendent, the plane took off at once for Milingimbie and Elcho Island. The Commonwealth Aerial Medical Service was most efficient in its ministry to both races, and I found that all missions along the coast were connected by wireless with Service headquarters in Darwin.

Goulburn Island Mission, an hour's flight to the south-east, was the tidiest mission I had ever seen. Fruit and vegetable gardens, fowl-yards, and piggery were kept in perfect condition by the aboriginal people—all full-bloods—under the direction of the missionary in charge, the Rev Alf Ellison. The people, although fewer than two hundred in number, represented five tribes, with varying languages. But this seemed to offer no bar to peaceful co-operative living.

Late one afternoon we crowded into a single-engined plane— and left for Darwin, a journey of one and three-quarter hours, instead of three days by sea. It was a splendid flight, with the wind behind us, though I found it more eerie than in a large aircraft. We were never more than two thousand feet from the ground, and we could readily follow details. We saw the holes in the sand and mud made by the water buffaloes, and we saw a group of the animals moving fast. The pilot said that they were certainly being driven from behind; he pointed out various buffalo-hunters' homes; they looked very desolate places. We looked down on many islands of varying sizes for the whole of that northern coast is broken by many tidal rivers that flow far inland. All the way we were flying over Arnhem Land just inland from the sea.

Arnhem Land in 1951 was estimated to have a population of between two thousand and three thousand aborigines, but it was evident that more and more of the younger people were making their way to Darwin every year. The pioneer missions on the Arnhem Land Reserve had done good work, but there was great need for trading posts to be set up along the coasts of the Reserve from which welfare patrols could make contact with the tribes. At such trading posts the aborigines could trade crocodile skins, turtle shell, baler shell, trepang, and the beautiful baskets and mats the women make from the pandanus palm. In exchange they could get calico, needles, fishing-gear, skinning knives, axes and tomahawks, files, tobacco, and foodstuffs. Kyle

Little was the pioneer in this policy, and it was most unfortunate that he was not encouraged. The Government should strive to provide employment for the aborigines in their own country, employment in which the natives themselves could find satisfaction.

During this visit in 1951 it was very evident to me that aborigines in Darwin were becoming conscious of the vast difference between their wage and that of the white man. Natives employed by the Government were still receiving only two pounds a week, which even with extras was not enough for independent living. There was no minimum wage in private employment. Wages for adult aborigines on cattle stations were grossly unfair. A pound a week on credit with rations and cheap tobacco was not a wage at all. When I made inquiries it was admitted that some stations were not even paying this meagre award.

Australians hate the word slavery in connection with aborigines, but it must be recognized that in countries where slavery does exist the slaves are at least generally well fed, well clothed, and well cared for. There can be no security for native workmen and their families until wages and living conditions are vastly improved and defaulting employers prosecuted. Treatment of aborigines on some stations was better than it had been in the past but scorn and contempt were still too often the lot of the dark-skinned workers. Owners who lived on and managed their stations tended to treat the aborigines better than did managers who had to make dividends for companies.

In Darwin at this time there was a large group of part-aboriginal people living independent and successful lives in the community. Of these the natural leader was Mr J. F. McGuinness, President of the Half-Caste Progressive Association of Darwin. At the end of 1951, he was a delegate from the North Australian Workers' Union to the Australian Trade Union Congress in Melbourne. In an impressive speech there he made two pleas: that part-aborigines be given full citizen rights, and that full-bloods be given the "right to survive as a race and to be treated as human beings."

Fatherless half-caste children were at that time segregated on islands; at Melville Island under the Roman Catholic Church, and at Croker Island under the Methodist Church. As a general rule half-caste babies born in the country west and south-west of Darwin went to Melville Island, and those born east and south-east of Darwin went to Croker Island. But they did not all go there at birth or soon afterwards. At the age of three to four months many half-caste babies in the native camps were taken from their full-blood mothers, brought to Darwin and placed under the care of the Aborigines Inland Mission, there to await final placing at a later date. I saw the babies in their cots; they were well cared for, but I was not satisfied that it was right to take these young babies from their mothers. It left the mothers broken-hearted, and it could not be in the interests of the children to become institutionalized so soon. It is recognized in all enlightened countries that early separation of mother and child should at all costs be avoided.

From Darwin I flew to Katherine by T.A.A., and by Connellan airline to Roper River. The atmosphere of this mission was very fine, and I was impressed by the splendid nursing work being done by the trained sister in a very primitive hospital building. The mission had not recovered from the utter wreckage of the flood, but plans were being made to erect modern buildings, including a hospital, on high ground about half a mile from the river. The mission, forty miles from the river mouth, had a contract to deliver mail to Groote Eylandt once a month.

The trip would take twenty-four hours or more according to the weather, which is usually rough. On one occasion that year the three white men on board were helplessly seasick, and for the worst eight hours the aboriginal seaman never once took his hand from the wheel. From Roper River I flew to Borroloola, a very small place on the Macarthur River, which flows into the Gulf of Carpentaria. Mr Ellis, the local officer of the Department of Native Affairs, was still excited over a huge groper he had caught, estimated to have weighed between two hundred and three hundred pounds.

Tennant Creek, the next place reached by plane, was simply a row of business premises; two hotels, school, post office, and police station arranged on either side of the Stuart Highway. The Government Hospital and the houses were set back from the road on the eastern side. Tennant Creek had no local water supply apart from rainwater in tanks, and further supplies had to be carted from six miles away. The whole place was dependent on the goldmines. The local aborigines had long since been removed to clear the way for the white man's profits.

Next day we flew to Alice Springs, where I met many old friends of both races and had a talk with Mr W. McCoy, head of the Native Affairs Branch there. It was heartening to hear from him that the owner of one cattle station near Alice Springs was setting a fine example by paying five pounds a week to his aboriginal stockmen and providing adequate housing.

I was greatly impressed with St Mary's Hostel, which had been the Lady Gowrie recreation centre for women of the forces during the second World War. Here Sister Eileen Heath of the Church of England had under her care fifty-seven part-aboriginal girls and boys. They were splendidly housed and cared for, the whole atmosphere being one of home life. The children attended the Alice Springs State school.

At the hospital I was very warmly welcomed by the Matron and Sisters. Sister O'Keefe, whom I knew well, took me to the native ward, which was her special charge. Polly from Erna-bella was still a patient, following amputation of her right leg. Her husband Punch I also knew very well; he was getting two pounds a week and his keep for growing vegetables in the hospital garden while his wife was under treatment. When Punch saw me in the distance he became quite excited, called my name, and with face beaming hurried over and took my hand. Then he introduced me to the other gardener.

This happy time at the hospital brought to an end a most satisfying visit to the Territory.

Adelaide's part-aborigines will always remember 31 August 1953 as a red-letter day. In the previous eighteen months several of the young people had shown ability in addressing small gatherings arranged by the Aborigines Advancement League of South Australia, of which I was then the President. The time had come for a wider appeal, and, to the consternation of some of my friends, I booked the Town Hall. But once the surprise was over, everyone, native and white alike, worked with a will. A town hall meeting to be addressed by aborigines was "news," and so the meeting received great publicity from the Press and the broadcasting stations.

It was held on the coldest and wettest night of the year, but the hall was crowded in every part. The programme included singing, and the playing of instruments by aborigines of different ages, speeches, and finally a film of the Ernabella Mission. It was a great honour to be chairman at such a historic gathering.

All did well, but the addresses by three men and two young women made the deepest impression. Without any resentment and in excellent English they told of the disabilities under which their people lived. Perhaps most memorable of these disabilities was related by an eighteen-year-old lad down from Alice Springs for education and training. He told the packed audience that he and his part-aboriginal friends had been refused the right to sit down with white people in the dining car of the north-south railway train.

Another matter brought forward by a young woman was the fact that two of her friends, fully qualified to start a nursing career, had been turned away from a public hospital to which they had applied for training. The matron had advised them to go north to Alice Springs and seek work nursing their own people. Fortunately this particular injustice was soon righted. The Press gave great publicity to the matter, and that same hospital has since trained part-aboriginal girls and has appointed several of them as ward-sisters.

The significance of that town hall meeting lay in the fact that part-aboriginal people, with encouragement, were prepared to speak and act for themselves. This roused great public sympathy, and was undoubtedly responsible for the rapid righting of some of the social wrongs of which they spoke.

A few months later Adelaide welcomed Her Majesty Queen Elizabeth, and Prince Philip. A unique group who came to Adelaide to join in the celebrations were twenty young tribal men and women from Ernabella, a thousand miles away. To them all it was an amazing experience: great buildings, busy highways, public transport, crowds of people massed together, all made up an astonishing sight. To those of us who knew the environment from which they came their behaviour was a lesson in poise and dignity. Their four-part singing, unselfconscious and perfectly balanced, gave delight wherever it was heard. They returned completely unspoiled, and true to their tribal tradition of sharing they carried home gifts for their friends and relatives. What they talked of most on their return was not buildings, crowds, nor even the Royal visitors, but the vastness of the sea.

The Federal Government arranged that the artist Namatjira and another aboriginal should be presented to Her Majesty, a tacit recognition that the members of their race as well as ours were loyal subjects and had a right to share in all the privileges traditionally inherent in British citizenship. But this gesture excellent in itself by no means heralded a new era of justice for aborigines, as the case of Jimmy Gwiethoona illustrates. For within months of Her Majesty's visit to Western Australia a Coroner's inquest found that an aboriginal had died at Merridin, Western Australia, as a result of a blow from a police constable. Here follows a record of the inquest.

> An Inquisition taken at Merridin within the State of Western Australia this 26th day of August 1954 (and by adjournment on 17th and 18th day of August 1954) by me Theodore Russell, a Coroner for the said State by law authorised to inquire: Why, where, and after what manner Jimmy Gwiethoona came by his death.

The Coroner found that:

> (a) Jimmy Gwiethoona died at Merridin District Hospital on 5th July 1954 from subdural haemorrhage received on 3rd July at Nungarin as a result of a blow delivered by R . . . K . . . L . . .
> (b) R . . . K . . . L . . . unlawfully killed Jimmy Gwiethoona.

According to the Bulletin of the Council for Aboriginal Rights:

> Gwiethoona, an aboriginal, was arrested at Nungarin about 9.30 on Saturday night, July 3, taken by Constable L — behind a shed "for questioning" and at about 10.30 p.m. put into a cell. A little later Constable L — put Crawley, another aboriginal, in the same cell. Not long after Crawley called "Come quick, boss" but Constable L — in evidence said that only when called a second time did he go to the cell. Gwiethoona was on his knees holding his face with both hands, and there was a pool of blood on the floor. Nothing was done that night. Next day when the sick man complained of pain in his face a police sergeant, who was brought to see him, prescribed bathing his face with salt and water. [Why this added cruelty?] The constable told the coroner that this was done to avoid the expense of getting

a doctor. At 8.30 p.m. the man complained again and he was taken by motor to a doctor at Kununoppin who examined him in the back of the car. He was to be kept warm, and if his condition got worse he was to be taken to Merridin District Hospital. Gwiethoona was then taken back to the cell.

On Monday at 10 a.m. in Court he was sentenced to fourteen days for soliciting liquor and fourteen days for resisting arrest. At 1.45 while eating dinner in his cell he collapsed and was taken to the Merridin District Hospital where fracture of both jaws and possible haemorrhage of brain was diagnosed. Post-mortem examination revealed "bilateral fracture of lower jaw, a subperiosteal haemorrhage size of a 2/- piece over right frontal region, some softening of brain underneath."

Westralian Aborigine, December 1954 stated:

> L — had been committed for trial on a charge of having unlawfully killed Gwiethoona. On Nov. 12th the Crown Law Department had announced it would not continue proceedings against L — because Gwiethoona had received his fatal injuries when he "fell over when resisting arrest."

The Aboriginal Coolbaroo League was dissatisfied with this pronouncement and asked the Minister for Justice, Mr Nulsen, to receive a deputation, but he replied he was too busy until after Parliament rose.

A Queenslander, Bill Confoy, later that year expressed himself as greatly shocked by the treatment of aborigines he had seen as he traversed the tributaries of the River Murray, and the Murray itself. He travelled from the end of August till the end of October 1954, and interviewed by the *News,* Adelaide, at the conclusion of his journey he said:

> Normally I'm not a bloke who gets on a soap-box, and until I made this trip I was as lethargic about the way we treat the aborigines as the next bloke. But I've changed. What I have seen makes me feel unclean and guilty, and never again will I point the finger at the American colour bar. The Americans' treatment of the Negroes makes them look like saints against us, and I

mean you and me and everyone else who inherited a stolen country and pushes the original owners out into a beaten hopeless nowhere. I've seen natives living in tin huts we "gave" them but I wouldn't use the huts as kennels for dogs. It's like this all along the river. The natives are fed on a starvation-rate basis; they are clothed like beggars; they are placed in a position where they're forced to hang around the streets doing nothing, and as a result get into drinking trouble, when we fling them into gaol. We are assisting the aborigines to fast become a race lost from the face of the earth. Any thieving that goes on along the rivers I've been through is automatically "blamed on the niggers." We deny them all representation in the Houses of our Parliaments. Near Bourke I saw people dragging the bodies of three aborigines from the river where I heard they'd drowned the day before running away from the police. Did that story get to the papers? How silly it must sound when I say all this and then tell you that the best-spoken man I met along the way down was a full-blooded, self-taught black man.

It was a relief to learn that cruelty to aborigines did not always pass unnoticed or go unpunished in the Queen's dominions. At Darwin on 15 December 1954 two pastoralists, brothers aged thirty-two and twenty-nine, were each sentenced to six months imprisonment and each fined four hundred pounds for having whipped and assaulted four men and one woman. A drover aged twenty-five was fined fifty pounds for wounding an aboriginal with a horse-whip.

But these sentences riled some station owners and managers.

The blacks will become too cheeky. If they are given a crack to make them work, or a kick in the pants they are likely to report it to the police. The only way to work niggers is to show superiority and authority.
Can't understand how white men could make such a mistake as letting the blacks get to the police. They should have shot the niggers.

In October 1956 with my wife I flew to the west coast of South Australia and found the outlook for aborigines there very unsatisfactory. We met some fine families of part-aborigines

104

living independently in various districts. But the greater number of both full-bloods and part-aborigines were congregated at two places—the Koonibba Mission at Penong, and Yalata Mission at Colona, both under the Evangelical Lutheran Church.

The atmosphere at Koonibba was depressing in the extreme, with native housing dark and ill-ventilated. Such segregated and substandard living would never help aborigines to face the outside world with confidence. They should be suitably housed in the many small townships of the country west of Ceduna so that the men could get regular work and wages and the children attend local State schools.

The semi-tribal natives, mostly of the full-blood, then living at Yalata, had been transported there in 1952 by the South Australian Government. They had been brought from the Ooldea Mission settlement, which was close to Maralinga, the area selected as an atomic testing ground. Tests had in fact been made there in September 1956, just prior to our visit, and residents spoke of the heavy blasts.

An arrangement had been made between the Government and the Evangelical Lutheran Church by which, in return for definite benefits, the Church was to provide education and spiritual guidance. At the time of our visit no education had yet been started, and three years later school was being conducted in the open as long as the teacher could keep the children interested. The teacher was travelling in a caravan; one could not by any stretch of imagination call this education.

Education and improved technical training for their children has always been a most important objective in the minds of thoughful part-aborigines. In 1946 I had been approached by three young aboriginal citizens, who asked me to help them get a meeting place they could call their own. It was arranged that they should place their ideas before the Aborigines Advancement League of South Australia, and after hearing them the League agreed to support their scheme.

Ten years of steady effort by the League, whose membership has always been of both races, resulted in the purchase of a fine home in an Adelaide suburb. On 19 November 1956 it was officially opened, well furnished and completely free of debt, by His Excellency, Air Vice-Marshal Sir Robert George, at that time Governor of South Australia. In 1960 it was necessary to extend the accommodation, and in an appeal for five thousand pounds the Government gave half the amount. The home accommodates seventeen part-aboriginal girls from the country who are furthering their education in Adelaide. It also retains a room for aboriginal women who may need temporary accommodation. Some of the schoolgirls are being supported by their own people, but the majority are maintained by the Government of South Australia while they remain at the hostel.

Social acceptance of the part-aboriginal, towards which the hostel was making a significant contribution, was seriously challenged the following year by the operation of a "consorting clause." This was a clause included in the Police Offences Act 1953 South Australia. The clause had made it an offence for any non-aboriginal habitually to consort with an aboriginal, but any operation of the clause had largely passed unnoticed until early in 1957. In February of that year, however, a flagrant case was brought to my notice.

A long-established friendship of two men and their families living in the same street at Victor Harbor was challenged. The two men, a white man and a part-aboriginal, were travelling in the latter's car when a constable stopped the car and asked to see the aboriginal driver's licence. The policeman then drew the white man aside and informed him that he was committing an offence by "consorting with a native." A great deal of indignation and real hurt in the community was felt over the whole affair. A moving tribute to the part-aboriginal is a letter in my possession which was written to him next day by the railway gang of which he was union representative. It assures him that:

> We are proud to work and keep company with you, and at any time you are welcome to our homes and our table. We appreciate your loyalty to us as our Union representative, a duty you carried out without prejudice. All this is in keeping with our Christian faith.

Then follow thirteen signatures.

During investigations other cases came to light, and public sentiment was strongly roused. The Aborigines Advancement League of South Australia organized a petition to have the clause repealed, and it was supported by Churches and leading organizations of citizens. The petition was presented to Parliament on 19 June 1958, and the clause was repealed shortly afterwards.

10

The Musgraves Again

EIGHTEEN YEARS HAD passed since my trip through the Aborigines Central Reserve in 1939. The contrast to the earlier trip was acute. A fast car now took us over graded roads where before we had needed the slow-moving camels in the trackless bush. For the reserve had now been radically altered by the establishment of the rocket range and the leasing of certain areas to mining interests. Traversing the Musgraves and the Mann Ranges we visited the mining camp at Mt Davies in the Tomkinson Range and went on to the Blackstone Range in Western Australia. Here was situated the headquarters of the West Mining Company.

From these two centres prospecting parties went forth every morning into the surrounding hills in the hope of striking nickel-bearing rock. At Blackstone there were well-appointed homes, laboratories with every requisite for research in mining, and an air-strip from which aeroplanes flew to survey the more distant parts of the reserve. This was the Great Central Reserve for Aborigines in 1957!

In mid-winter 1958 we were again at Ernabella Mission and found everything in good heart. This year in addition to a basic diet there was specialized feeding for mothers, babies, toddlers, and schoolchildren. The tribe had been vaccinated by the South Australian Public Health Department against tuberculosis, poliomyelitis, Asian influenza, diphtheria, whooping cough, and tetanus.

I had been asked to give further injections against Asian influenza, and much of our time—after a day or two's work at the mission clinic—was spent in travelling through the beautiful Musgrave country to the various outlying sheep camps. Here were groups of aborigines living with their families for some months at a time shepherding the sheep. Most of the people fully understood the purpose of the injections I was giving and were most co-operative. But it was amusing to be met with a flat refusal by my old friend and guide of the 1939 trip, Tjuintjara. He was laughingly accused by the others of fearing the needle, but perhaps he felt he was immune to white man's sicknesses.

One of these trips took us out to Turner's Well, and here were camped Nganyintja with her husband and four children. As soon as she saw my wife getting down from the truck, she handed her tiny baby boy to his toddler sister and ran at top speed over the red sand to welcome and embrace her. It was a moving and unique experience to find her so completely uninhibited in her warmth of expression. She was not made self-conscious by the contrast between the life she had led in our home from time to time and the primitive surroundings where she now lived so happily. For at these camps the only concession to the white man's way of life was the adoption of some simple clothes and a blanket.

I saw on this visit a most interesting medical case. A young lad in his teens, in the process of initiation into tribal manhood, must keep out of sight of the tribe. One of these "nyingkas," feeling ill and weak, came to the mission late one night and sought out the nursing sister; he complained of his back. Sister brought him to me for diagnosis. My full medical report is too detailed to include here, but he had a raised area three-quarters of an inch high and three-quarters of an inch wide, extending from the middle of his spine straight across the left side of his back. Light pressure caused blood and pus to exude from two spots on the swelling over the spine.

This was a case of yaws, and I immediately gave an injection of two million units of penicillin, with another million to be given later if the lad remained in the vicinity. He immediately went back into the seclusion of the bush. When seen by Sister about two months later he was given the second injection of penicillin. In place of the long thickened area she found that there was by then only a fine fibrous cord.

Aborigines numbering between three hundred and fifty and four hundred were now living more or less permanently at the Mission, though they were completely free to come and go, as they always had been. They were settling in to the new way of life with apparent ease and happiness. But the increased number of people brought a problem—the growing scarcity of firewood in the vicinity of the Mission. The mission natives were still living in wurlies in the open, and firewood in these conditions was a necessity.

Another problem was the number of young men who had been educated at the school, but for whom work was not available. Groups of men were repeatedly asking for work. Lack of work is not peculiar to Ernabella; there are pockets of unemployed full-blood men throughout the interior. This is a major problem, for regular satisfying employment will be difficult to provide in the dry inland, and no tribe is happy or contented away from its own tribal land.

Ernabella was threatened the following year with another outbreak of measles. On Friday evening of 20 February 1959 at eight-fifteen a telegram was phoned to my home in Adelaide— "A case of measles at the Mission." This meant immediate action to prevent an epidemic of measles spreading through the Pitjantjatjara tribe. Gamma globulin serum would have to reach Ernabella, a thousand miles away, without delay, for if the serum is to be effective contacts must be treated within three days of an outbreak. In spite of the late hour, my appeal for help from Public Service Departments, so often maligned, met with instant response. Trans Australia Airlines offered to take the medical parcel on the early morning plane to Alice Springs. The Commonwealth Department of Health was closed, but my phone call was answered by the emergency Sister at her home. At once, though it was late evening, she went to headquarters, phoned me the amount available, packed the serum and delivered it to the T.A.A. City office.

G.P.O. telegraph then took my telegram. It was medically important, I said, that my message should reach Alice Springs in time for relaying on the early morning call to the mission by the radio network. The operator in charge was most co-operative and put the message through to Alice Springs. In my wire I requested that the Flying Doctor deliver the serum as soon as possible. He did, and twenty hours after I received notification of the outbreak the serum arrived at the mission. Contacts were immediately given injections, and an epidemic was prevented.

On the way to Ayers Rock a few months later we passed through Coober Pedy. The place had recently suffered an epidemic of influenza, with the death of several aborigines. We had stayed there for some hours on our way north and found the aborigines, many of them part white, living in earth-floor humpies, receiving no education and no instruction in hygiene. A departmental officer had inspected the situation and had stated that the aborigines were too primitive to stay in homes. At the native camp I found three aborigines known to me who had definitely lived in houses before going to Coober Pedy.

The place had changed greatly since my visit in 1935. There were now two general stores with rival petrol pumps; one of the stores provided meals and beds. With the high price of opal, white people and aborigines had gone to the field in increasing numbers.

Another opal field had been discovered in South Australia a hundred miles north of Port Augusta—Andamooka. Living conditions for the community of three hundred aborigines and two hundred whites were better than at Coober Pedy, and modern equipment was being used by white men with capital. Complaints were made by aboriginal opal gougers that some buyers had been unfair in the amounts paid them for opal. An old native of about seventy-five years stated publicly that he and two others, one of whom I know well, had been paid fifty pounds for an opal matrix weighing over a hundredweight, on the understanding that more money would be sent if the matrix sold well. They received nothing further, though it was reported in *The Advertiser* of 20 June 1959 that the find was sold overseas for a huge figure.

The United Nations Association of South Australia celebrated in December 1958 the tenth anniversary of the Universal Declaration of Human Rights. At a symposium arranged in this connection I urged that the United Nations Association of Australia should use its influence to see that the Declaration applied to our aborigines. In warmly supporting me the ex-President, Dr Van Abbe, said that the "Declaration was being trampled on every day with regard to aborigines."

The truth of this statement was even then being illustrated in Alice Springs, where a white man aged thirty-two was arrested for alleged assault on a native at Papunya native settlement, north-west of Alice Springs. He was remanded on bail of twenty-five pounds to appear at Alice Springs Police Court on 12 January 1959. He failed to appear. According to a Press report the Police Prosecutor told the stipendiary magistrate that four men, including the accused, who was foreman carpenter at the native welfare settlement, had gone to a native camp to remove a native. "He was run down by a Land-Rover, thrashed with a pick handle, and given a thorough hiding."

A warrant was issued for the arrest of the accused, but it was found that he had left the Territory. Extradition proceedings were not taken, and as the case never came to trial it is impossible to affirm that the foreman was guilty of the offence. The native had been taken to hospital, however, where he was examined and found to be suffering from bruising and a fractured rib. He was discharged on 25 December.

Human rights were constantly ignored in the anomalies that arose from varying State and Federal laws on aborigines. By now the Northern Territory citizenship ordinance of 1953 was taking effect, but part-aborigines who were citizens in the Northern Territory lost their status when they crossed State boundaries. Stockmen droving cattle overland from the Territory to West Australia and Queensland were the chief sufferers, but the disability also affected those crossing into South Australia. This anomaly still exists.

Even with his newly acquired status in the Northern Territory the part-aboriginal is not necessarily protected against discrimination as the following story shows.

In October 1959 a young part-aboriginal drover, Richard Joseph Smith, was walking out of a shop in the main street of Alice Springs. He was suddenly grabbed by a powerful black-tracker in uniform, thrown to the ground, stood on and kicked. "Then a utility pulled up," said an eye-witness, "and two white policemen jumped out. The black policeman kept on kicking the young man." Smith started to get into the utility when led there, but was grabbed by the leg and thrown in "head over heels." One policeman got in beside him, but the tracker was still kicking Smith, unprotected by the policeman, as the utility drove off.

But for the fact that a Melbourne woman witnessed the whole scene and complained, nothing would have been heard of it. Actually a charge of drunkenness was laid against Smith by the police, but when the case came on the police applied for permission to withdraw the charge. Mrs Katherine Foley, of Melbourne, had described the incident as "the most disgraceful thing I have ever seen."

Counsel for the defendant objected to withdrawal of the charge. The magistrate dismissed the case against Smith without hesitation and ordered the prosecutor to forward a copy of the deposition to the "appropriate authorities," indicating that he felt there was a strong possibility of further action.

That such an incident could happen at the end of 1959 in Alice Springs is an illustration of the fact that social justice and equality often lag far behind the legal enactments providing for them. Several years had passed since the operation of the Northern Territory Ordinance recognizing the irrevocable citizenship of all part-aboriginal people of the Territory.

No white man in Alice Springs would have been subjected to such treatment by the police as was suffered by Richard Joseph Smith.

In the Northern Territory new regulations governing employment of full-bloods became operative early in October 1959. The ordinance stated that employers must be licensed, and must pay fixed wages which must not be affected if time were lost because of wet weather. The award specified the number of hours to be worked and that the aborigines were eligible for overtime: that they were to get two weeks' annual leave and a week's sick leave on full pay. A week's notice was to be given on either side for termination of the job. Casual labour was rated at two pounds a week, and women employed as domestics were to get one pound. In addition a man was to receive fifteen shillings a week for clothing, plus food and tobacco, and provision of food and clothing was to be made for one wife and one child.

The most radical regulation applied to housing. Married workers with their families were to be provided with individual houses which were to have a floor area of not less than sixty square feet for each person as well as sixty square feet for a kitchen, and a six-foot wide veranda. Windows and doors, weatherproof walls and floors, and adequate basic furniture were to be provided. Single men and women were to be accommodated in barracks with kitchens and ablution blocks.

The new regulations were openly and hotly opposed by many pastoralists, and it was evident that without their co-operation little improvement would result. The vast distances of Australia's outback make the policing of such matters extremely difficult. To date the regulations have been flouted more than

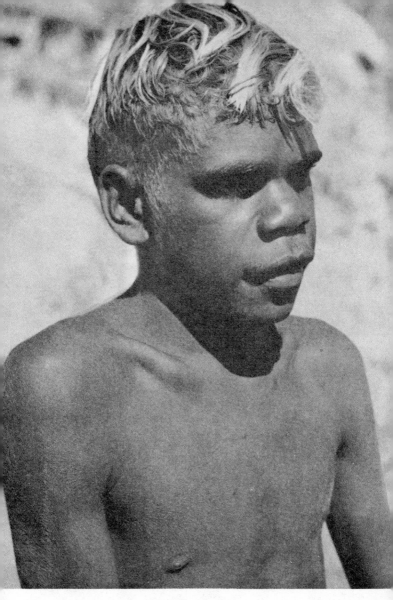

Ernabella schoolboy

Boy from the Pitjantjatjara tribe, Musgrave Ranges.

obeyed in spite of the fact that pastoralists make very considerable profits and are exempt from income tax. In contrast to the cry of so many pastoralists that "aborigines are not worth a decent wage" is the statement by a Darwin industrialist who employed in 1959 forty-three full-blood aborigines. The job was the shovelling and bagging of six hundred tons of salt, and the employment lasted over four weeks. "We paid them ten shillings an hour for seven days a week to work hard. And they did work hard. They were completely satisfactory, and we will employ them again next year."

In the legislative field the Federal Government took another important step when it announced that from 2 February 1960 its Social Service benefits would be extended to all aborigines except those who were nomadic or primitive. This decision of the Federal Government ended one of the major discriminations against the aborigines of Australia. For prior to 1960 aboriginal people, and part-aborigines with a preponderance of aboriginal blood were not eligible for old age, invalid, or widows' pensions, maternity allowance, or tuberculosis allowance, unless they had been granted exemption from the Aborigines Act of the particular State where they resided.

This new Federal legislation was hailed with great satisfaction by the many people who had advocated it over the years. But very soon certain groups of aborigines felt a good deal of disillusionment when they found that pensions were not paid directly to them as to white people. This was the case when they were living on a Government settlement or a mission and were held to be receiving in food or rent the equivalent of the greater part of the pension.

It was said by a spokesman of the Social Services Department that payments would be made by managers of Government settlements and superintendents of missions; that aborigines would be allowed about ten shillings a week spending money, and the remainder of the pension would be available for amenities "or as the manager sees fit."

Strong exception has been taken in many quarters to the retention by Government settlements or missions of the major portion of the pension, but it must be remembered that similar provision is made with regard to pensioners of the white race living in aged people's homes. The clause "as the manager sees fit" however, is obviously open to abuse.

In Canberra on 16 March 1960, Mr Clyde Cameron, M.P., stated that aged pensioners at a Government aboriginal settlement in South Australia were being paid their pension in the form of a ration of bread, butter, groceries, and vegetables with fifteen shillings a week in cash. He said that no statement was given to them of the cost of the goods supplied. He asked the Social Services Minister, Mr Roberton, to see that aborigines were given their full pension to spend in a way they saw fit. One of the aborigines from the settlement in question made strong "protest against pension payments being made to the Aborigines Department. We feel that as electors of both the Federal and State Parliaments pensions should be paid direct to the aborigines concerned."

The exclusion of nomadic natives from Social Service benefits was understandable, but it was deeply disturbing to read only ten days after the Minister announced extension of benefits to aborigines, that about two hundred nomads had arrived in a starving condition at a cattle station a hundred and fifty miles from Alice Springs. The plight of nomadic aborigines can be desperate in time of drought, and the law has not yet found a way to succour them.

In the same year, 1960, one of the welfare officers of the Northern Territory gave a pitiful picture of hardship when reporting on a welfare patrol near the border of Western Australia. He said that three aborigines spent an entire day hunting for food and returned at dusk exhausted—with one three-foot sñake, one seven-inch lizard, and one small goanna. These would be shared with their relatives.

A thorough investigation into desert living in certain parts of Australia, and reports to the relevant parliaments should be undertaken without delay. Welfare patrols would then surely be greatly extended to ensure that all our aborigines have at least the bare human right of adequate food.

11

Slow Progress

IN MAY 1960 the Minister for Territories, Mr Paul Hasluck, kindly enabled me to visit the new settlements the Federal Government was developing for the aboriginal people of the Northern Territory. The purpose of these settlements was to enable aborigines in varying degrees of de-tribalization to acquire a working knowledge of many phases of life in our civilization. The gradual adoption of a settled and "western" way of life was planned with the guidance of trained welfare officers, instructors, and nurses. Each of the six settlements I visited was designed to assist from three hundred to six hundred native people; the beginning of housing was dealt with by the construction of prefabricated aluminium houses—a single room with a six-foot veranda on three sides. A second stage in housing —cement brick houses—was also under way.

Each settlement had a school, a pre-school centre, a modern hospital, and well-equipped central kitchen and canteen. Perhaps the settlement which had gone the furthest in modern training and equipment was Warrabri, two hundred and forty miles north of Alice Springs. As well as the Wailbris, this served the Warramunga people who had been moved from Tennant Creek in 1933. Here there was a domestic science teacher helping with training in hygiene and home management. The hospital had its infant welfare clinic, and the two Sisters in charge were training young native women as nurses and nurse-aids. There was an industrial training centre where carpentry, plumbing, welding, sheet metal work, black-smithing, brickmaking, and saddling were being taught. There was also a garage workshop, where aborigines were taught the mechanics of a motor and its management. The success of the whole venture was illustrated by the fact that the Settlement's plumber was a full-blood aboriginal on a weekly wage of ten pounds.

At one of the other settlements, Yuendumu, I was interested to see natives cutting stone from a quarry; there was limestone also on this property, and the Superintendent was hopeful that the natives would soon begin to build their own houses. This is now taking place.

My greatest interest was naturally in the forty-five thousand square mile Pintubi Reserve which includes Papunya and Haast Bluff. This was the area in the south-west corner of the Territory which I had patrolled by camel with Pastor Albrecht in 1936. These Pintubi folk had been naked nomads, untouched by civilization except for Pastor Albrecht's occasional camel-patrols. It was very heart-warming to be recognized after twenty-four years by some of the people. In particular Tjararu, the active lad of eleven years old who had attached himself to me in 1936, knew me at once and took me with great pride to see his wife and five children. Though living was less advanced here at Papunya than at the older settlements training was going ahead. There were a hundred and forty schoolchildren, and instruction-employment was found for at least ninety men and forty-two women. At the cattle project near Haast Bluff, twenty-four men and thirteen women were employed. Housing was only just starting at Papunya, but the whole area was provided with electric light and power.

I returned to Adelaide with a sense of satisfaction that at last a comprehensive and long-range policy for aborigines had been worked out. But there is an inherent weakness in the scheme. The aborigines, divorced from their tribal life and the discipline of their own culture, are forced to accept laws and sanctions they cannot readily understand.

The South Australian Government at this time decided to establish a cattle station in the western Musgrave Ranges to train and employ tribal aborigines. It is to be hoped that the Government's venture will eventually extend westward to the Tomkinson Ranges, where there is excellent cattle country. The aim should be to train and settle the young men with their wives and families in their own country. At the end of the first ten years of the Ernabella Mission I claimed that adequately trained Pitjantjatjara natives could in future be responsible for the development of this whole north-west corner of South Australia. The extension of the Government's Musgrave Park scheme could make this a reality in the not too distant future.

Government policy for aborigines was still further advanced when Commonwealth and State Ministers met in conference in Canberra on 26 and 27 January 1961 to discuss the "assimilation" of aborigines. Ministers responsible for aboriginal welfare in all States attended the conference and set out an excellent charter to serve as a standard throughout Australia. Some of the main points stressed by the Ministers were that the community should:

Encourage nomadic natives to adopt a more settled life.

Provide better housing, food, schooling, vocational training, and jobs.

Educate aboriginal children in normal schools wherever possible.

Improve housing and hygienic standards on Government settlements, missions, rural properties, and in towns.

Teach aborigines to use improved housing.

Train aborigines to help the advancement of their own people by training them as teaching, nursing, and medical assistants, patrol officers, and welfare officers.

Encourage aboriginal sporting activity.

Remove restrictive or protective legislation as soon as the capacity or advancement of the individual permitted.

Make people aware that assimilation was not possible unless advanced aborigines were accepted into the community without prejudice.

Unless all Governments in Australia move into action without delay along the lines of the Conference there will be very little benefit to the aborigines. How, even two months later, the Conference Charter was applied in Western Australia was told by the Sydney *Bulletin* of 5 April 1961, under the heading "Lesson for Primitives," I quote in full:

When two primitive aborigines and a retinue of children left the never-never country of Western Australia Canning stock route and travelled westwards into the empire of the Kimberley cattle kings they knew nothing of the white man's ways or of his justice. Their hunting grounds had failed and they were looking for food, which they found among the scrub cattle grazing in the pindan. They fed so well that a police party, complete

117

with Land-Rover and native trackers, set out from Fitzroy Crossing for Christmas Creek station to investigate the illegal killing of cattle. When found by the police the killers dropped their spears and ran from the Land-Rover in fear. But the two men were brought back to Fitzroy Crossing to stand trial. Next day they appeared before the local magistrate dressed as they were captured—in khaki loincloths tied round their waists, and with their knotted hair hanging down to their shoulders.

The magistrate remanded them for eight days to give the West Australian Native Welfare Department an opportunity of representing them. When the case was again heard they had been washed and shaved and provided with a defence counsel in the person of a Native Welfare officer who could not speak their language. The serious charge of illegal killing of cattle was reduced to one of being in possession of beef suspected of being stolen. The sentence—£50 fine or 50 days imprisonment. The time—March 20, 1961.

It would be interesting to know what happened to the wives and children during the seven weeks the men were in gaol.

Nor did the Canberra Conference have much practical significance in the uplifting of aborigines in Queensland, judging by recent reports on Cape York Peninsula. Although the Queensland Government is legally and morally responsible for the large number of aborigines in the Peninsula, and although missions have been in existence in the area since the end of last century, the plight of the natives there is reported to be pitiful in the extreme. In April 1961 the Bishop of Carpentaria, the Rt Rev John Matthews, visited Adelaide on his way to Alice Springs, which is part of his diocese. His charges include more than twelve hundred aborigines at Lockhart River, Edward River, and Mitchell River Missions.

"The aborigines of Cape York Peninsula settlements are the most neglected for want of finance of any in Australia," he said. "Last October I walked round Lockhart Mission. My head bowed lower at every step because of what I saw." The Bishop went on to say that the Missions were giving education to the aborigines in primitive schools not under the care of the State education authorities, and when asked about assimilation he told the *Advertiser* "If the Government wants assimilation it must give these people an opportunity to learn to live with dignity."

The Anglican, a Church of England independent journal, on 28 April 1961 published material with the concurrence of the Bishop. It described food as "totally inadequate in nutriment and quantity"; housing as in a terrible condition, with little or no washing, bathing, or laundry facilities; sanitary conditions indescribable, with hookworm disease rife. From what I know of other missions in Cape York Peninsula it would seem that an independent commission of inquiry into Government and mission policy and practice in the Peninsula is called for.

Presbyterian missions in the same part of Australia had a new problem to face. The finding of bauxite in huge quantities on the shore of the Peninsula resulted in the Queensland Government leasing mission reserves to a powerful mining company, Comalco. This is dealt with in subsequent chapters.

An independent commission of inquiry such as I suggest might reveal not only inadequacies in their food or housing, but much room for improvement in the attitudes to and treatment of aborigines. In May 1961 a young aboriginal man, Jim Jacko, had been caned and transported from Hopevale Lutheran Mission, Cape York Peninsula, to Cooktown on the coast, there to await a steamer to take him via Cairns to the discipline of Palm Island.

At Cairns, not being under restraint, he made contact with a member of the Aborigines' Advancement League who in turn sought out W. Wallace, M.P. Mr Wallace ascertained from the police that there were no charges against Jacko. The resulting publicity led the Minister for Health and Home Affairs, Dr H. W. Noble, to order an open magisterial inquiry into the caning.

In August the report of the inquiry by visiting Justice J. O. Lee was released. The complaint was that the young man had left the mission with his sweetheart without permission. The youth was not charged with any offence nor brought before any court, and the Justice found the caning inexcusable.

A month before the Bishop of Carpentaria's tragic report on lack of finance for decent living for aborigines in Cape York

Peninsula a statement, startling in its contrast, came from the Federal Minister for Development, Senator Spooner. He said in a television interview on 26 March 1961 that millions of pounds were to be spent "within a few months" on new arterial all-weather roads across Cape York Peninsula to transport cattle and mineral wealth to Queensland rail and roadheads.

And so, in 1961, one hundred and seventy-three years after our coming to Australia, our nation is able to spend millions of pounds in opening up Cape York Peninsula for the better accommodation of the cattleman and the miner. How much have we spent in opening up a better life for the fellow human beings we have supplanted in that same part of Australia?

The vital importance of education for aborigines was now recognized by both Federal and State Governments. In 1961 the Federal Government announced its plan to have every child of school age in the Territory attending school within three years. Already many aboriginal children there were being educated, but about two thousand were still without any opportunity for education. The children were therefore to be catered for on a progressive scale; at first they were to attend a special school, and after some training they would be sent to an ordinary public school alongside white children.

Five of these full-blood children who had already attended a special school were sent in February 1962 to Elliott public school about five hundred miles north of Alice Springs. But when they arrived at school all seven white children were withdrawn by their parents, who appealed that the aboriginal children should not be allowed to attend. The Administrator for the Northern Territory, Mr Nott, replied that aboriginal children could not be excluded, and that all children would be inspected daily for cleanliness. Even then some white children were kept away, and the schoolmistress herself, in a letter to *The Advertiser* said, "I do not consider these particular children are suitable playmates for my girls," and continued that her objection was based not on colour "but on the way of life," and "the fact that they have their own school at Newcastle Waters."

Are these children for ever to be segregated in "their own school?" And are they to be denied the very best introduction to our "way of life"—lessons and play with our own children?

120

In the same year the South Australian and Queensland Governments decided to make education of aborigines the full responsibility of their State Education Departments.

Increasing Government sense of responsibility for aborigines showed in the Federal Government's appointment of an all-party Select Committee on Voting Rights of Aborigines. This Committee travelled throughout Australia in 1961 collecting evidence from more than three hundred witnesses, nearly half being of aboriginal descent. The evidence covered "education, housing, employment, the drink problem, and questions relating to policies in respect of missions and settlements and the welfare of the native generally. In their own words the natives placed before the committee the hopes and aspirations not only of men but also of women of the aboriginal people." The committee reported to Parliament it was unanimous that all aborigines and Torres Strait Islanders should have the right to vote at Commonwealth elections without any reservations. And at the next session of Parliament a Bill was passed conferring these rights.

One of the most significant matters brought to light by the Committee is a memorandum from the Federal Attorney-General's Department to the Chief Electoral Officer that half-castes and others of lesser blood were not aboriginal natives within the meaning of Section 127 of the Constitution. Despite this the Committee "established the fact that thousands of such people in Queensland and Western Australia who are already integrated in the community and are not living in the tribal state, have the right to be enrolled and to vote at Commonwealth elections but are unaware of the fact." They have been eligible since 25 January 1929, when a definition of an aboriginal was set out in a memorandum of the Attorney-General's Department.

The limiting of the rights of citizenship by State legislatures was dealt with by the Minister for Territories, the Hon Paul Hasluck, in an address on "The Administration of Native Welfare," July 1961.

> It is a misconception to talk of giving citizenship to aborigines. The historical fact is that the exercise of their rights had been limited by legislation passed by Colonial, State or Territorial legislatures analogous to the way legislation limited the exercise of rights by other special classes of Australians, such as bankrupts, the

mentally afflicted, persons under 21 years of age, and a person declared to be an habitual drunkard. The process was not to "grant" them citizenship—that was a silly pretension by State Parliaments to powers which they did not have—but to repeal or modify the laws which applied only to aborigines or remove individuals of the aboriginal race from the operation of those laws.

How unwilling State Legislatures often are to "remove individuals from the operation of these laws!" In 1961, George Koolmaterie, a part-aboriginal tractor driver, applied to the Aborigines Protection Board of South Australia for exemption from the Aborigines Act. His application was refused. He appealed before a magistrate against this decision, and in evidence before the Court the Secretary of the Protection Board Mr C. E. Bartlett, himself admitted that Koolmaterie had controlled his own affairs all his life. He owned a car, and was employed at the ruling rate as a tractor driver.

In dismissing the appeal the Magistrate, D. L. Richards, said an applicant for exemption had to prove he could obtain food, shelter, and medical attention without help. He should have saved money for times when he might be unemployed; the appeal was refused because the magistrate considered the evidence fell short of establishing the requirements for exemption.

Evidently higher standards are required of aborigines than of other citizens! This case has been taken to the Australian Section of the International Commission of Jurists.

Also from South Australia comes another glaring illustration of discrimination under State laws. With a view to visiting Europe a young married couple applied for passports. But on 18 December 1961, the wife, a double-certificated nurse, a communicant member of a Christian Church, and a voter at State and Federal elections, received the following letter from the Aborigines Department, South Australia.

Dear Madam,
To facilitate the obtaining of your passport, the Aborigines Protection Board have today granted you a Limited Declaration of Exemption from the provisions of the Aborigines Act. In order to finalise this, will

you please forward by return of mail two photographs of yourself, head and shoulders only, approximately 2 ins x 2 ins in size?

The young couple, a European husband and part-aboriginal wife, naturally resented this communication. They had already supplied photographs to the Passport Office as is required of all travellers. But because of the wife's darker colour the Passport Office asked the Aborigines Department if they knew of any reason why she should not be allowed to travel. As the lady was a British subject and an Australian citizen this action on the part of a Commonwealth Department is difficult to understand.

Perhaps they knew that in South Australia all aborigines of any degree of aboriginal blood, unless exempted from the 1939 Aborigines Act, legally come under the control of the Aborigines Department no matter how fine their character, how high their academic status, or how advanced their development. This young woman had never had anything to do with the Aborigines Department at any time, being always an independent member of society, and she wrote to the Department for an explanation.

In reply she was informed that:

> Section 12 (1) of the Aborigines Act provides that it is an offence for any aborigine to be removed to any place beyond the State without the authority of the Board.

Resentment changed to indignation, and she asked me: "Who is removing me, have I no free will?"

This young woman is one of a great many advanced part-white aborigines who will not apply for exemption from the Aborigines Act because they believe they are citizens of the State by birth as well as citizens of Australia. To offer her a *Limited* Declaration of Exemption was adding insult to injury, for it is conditional on character, intelligence, and development, and can be revoked up to three years after its issue. The blame for this ignominy lies not so much with the Department's servants as with the State Parliament that allows an utterly out-dated, out-moded Act to remain on the statute book.

Only a few weeks after the incident just described a part-aboriginal woman, educated, trained, and a trusted member of the Federal public service, walked confidently into the office of a leading Australian life insurance society in a capital city with the intention of taking out a life policy. She was asked by an embarrassed member of the staff about her race, and was informed that the society did not accept aborigines. She agreed to his suggestion that she should discuss the matter with his senior officer and courageously stood her ground, perhaps giving him a new conception of an "aborigine."

Subsequently the manager informed me that their refusal was due to advice from their statistical department on the expectation of life of aborigines; that he was sorry for the hurt caused and would see if an exception could be made in her favour. This she would not have agreed to; she wanted nothing that did not include others of her race. It is only fair to record that she was accepted next day by an equally well-established society.

If their expectation of life is considered too poor for insurance, what a grim unspoken comment this is on our years of contact with the aboriginal race.

As a nation we enjoy a standard of living unsurpassed in the world today, and yet we must face the shameful fact that there is a minority group among us who lack recognition, acceptance, and sometimes even food.

These aboriginal people are no longer dying out—they are increasing every year and though we can never forget the dark history of their past suffering it is within our powers to write a different story for the future. Their children at least must inherit Australia equally with our children.

PART II

In the following chapter epitaphs I have used some of the statements most commonly heard about our aborigines in order to show that no race on earth has been more maligned.

12

Intelligence And Culture

"They haven't the white man's brain."

THE SCOTTISH EXPLORER Thomas Mitchell, at the conclusion of his fourth and longest expedition in the middle of the nineteenth century, wrote thus:

> It would ill become me to disparage the character of the aborigines, for one of that unfortunate race has been my guide, companion, counsellor and friend in the most eventful occasion during this Journey of Destiny.

Yuranigh was, he said,

> of the most determined courage and resolution. His intelligence, his judgement, rendered him so necessary to me that he was ever at my elbow, whether on foot or horseback. Confidence in him was never misplaced.

It is an interesting commentary on the times that Mitchell, anxious to have an aboriginal couple, a young man and woman, educated, had to admit it would be necessary to send them to another country for ten to twelve years. Education of Australian aborigines in 1850 and well into the twentieth century was regarded as an absurdity, and today few people realize that in mental potential aborigines are not behind us, and that given full respect and opportunity their performance would soon rise to our level though our civilization is alien to them.

The great majority of Australians still regard aborigines as an inferior race, incapable of development. According to the father of Dame Mary Gilmore, the development of the aborigines was brought nearly to a standstill by the rapid slaughtering they suffered a hundred years ago.

Mary Gilmore, in her *More Recollections,* wrote:

> In killing off the elder men and women who were the direct inheritors of the past, not only with its lore, but with the language of its lore, the result has been that only

the less educated (using the word in its best sense) were left to carry on what had been received from the ages. Further it is certain that instead of intellectual men being in a position to develop thought and explain it even to the white man, the perceptive energy of the tribal mind had to be given to the problem of escape from death and to the immediate needs of survival.

But despite what was lost much remained. Father Ernst Wurms, of Kew College, Melbourne, claims that the language of the Kimberley natives in Western Australia was harder to learn than French or German because of the variation of their grammar. It was not true, he said, that aborigines were able to think only in concrete forms; he had found abstract ideas among them.

Dr Donald Thomson, outstanding scientist and anthropologist, of Melbourne University, who lived for nearly seven years with the aborigines of Arnhem Land reported:

> They possess a rich and expressive language often with complex grammatical forms, and many natives employ a wider vocabulary and better choice of words than some educated white men. They possess a rich and elaborate mythology and religious and political codes and institutions which are adequate for their needs, and serve well for the regulation of conduct.

The Rev Dr Herman Nekes, a German priest and anthropologist, in the years 1935-38 lived at Beagle Bay in Australia's north-west, studying the local languages. With nine full-blood bush aborigines he sat at a table, asked questions, and compared the different answers. Each of the nine spoke a different tongue, yet after some months these nine men began to understand one another's language. Dr Nekes affirms that some of the most mentally alert began to use grammatical terms and discussed syntax, and months later dealt with phonetic symbols, explained the finer points of pronunciation and showed the difference between dialects that appeared similar.

Dr D. S. Davidson, Professor of Anthropology, University of Pennsylvania, stated that Australian aborigines were as intelligent as modern Americans.

> They have adjusted themselves to their environment as intelligently—sometimes I think more intelligently

Primitive children at school. Pitjantjatjara tribe, Musgrave Ranges.

Country near Ernabella. Spinifex in the foreground.

Pitjantjatjara children at play in the Eastern Musgraves.

Pitjantjatjara girls.

—than we have to ours. Just now they are in a struggle to survive the shock of their way of life and ours which is pressing in on them.

Dr Warner, of the Rockefeller Foundation, reported:

> I think the aborigine every bit as intelligent as the white man—the reason he has not correspondingly advanced is due to centuries of isolation.

The mathematical precision of the boomerang, as made by tribal natives for use and not by fringe-dwellers for sale, inspired the following statement by Oswald Spengler in *Form and Actuality*—

> The Australian natives, who rank intellectually as thorough primitives, possess a mathematical instinct . . . that as regards the interpretation of pure space is far superior to that of the Greeks. Their discovery of the boomerang can only be attributed to their having a sure feeling for numbers of a class that one should refer to the higher geometry. Accordingly—we shall justify the adjective later—they possess an extraordinarily complicated ceremonial and, for expressing degrees of affinity, such fine shades of language as not even the higher cultures can show.

Their intelligence is much in evidence in the practical issues of their everyday life. A man with a persistent bleeding point has been known to put a bull-ant on the vessel. It bites, and the flow of blood stops. He kills the ant and leaves the nippers on. Nothing is more nervously upsetting to an infant than to have an ant or a fly burrowing or buzzing in the depth of an ear. I have seen a white child hysterical with the buzzing until warm water was poured into the canal. But a mother in arid country has no water at hand to pacify her tribal baby. She will squirt milk from her breast into the ear; this clogs the insect and more milk washes it out.

A hungry boy one morning caught a bee that had alighted on a bush flower. To its hairy body he attached some eagle down, often carried by aborigines behind the ear, just enough to slow the bee's progress, and then let it go. The boy followed fast, keeping the bee in sight until it reached a dead tree. Here with an effort it raised itself to a hole in the trunk. After recovering his breath the boy climbed the tree and got his breakfast of honey. Aborigines have very acute sight and hearing, and their powers of observation are so highly trained that in knowledge of plants and animals, in reading signs on the ground, in forecasting weather, and in the management of fire in the bush, they stand alone.

Mary Gilmore has told in *Old Days, Old Ways,* how her parents were taught by the aborigines to make tan lotion from wattle bark for unbroken burns and scalds and how, with eucalyptus leaves in pits, they made vapour for chills and pains.

They have great ability in balanced choral singing, and several mission choirs have won outstanding praise for recorded performances. A children's choir from a mission in the Northern Territory took the major awards at a recent Eisteddfod. It is regrettable that the haunting beauty of tribal singing is now seldom heard at missions.

Perhaps too we have lost much of what they might have shared with us in other branches of art. In painting, carving, and in sculpture, individual aborigines have proved themselves outstanding. But the tragedy is that, in spite of our knowledge of unique cave drawings all over Australia, the race has never been encouraged to develop its powers; only here and there has the brilliance of an individual shone through.

Tribal people have their own way of telling the time—by the variations of the moon. For instance, nomads who have been living for many months far off in the bush will arrive at a mission on Christmas eve or early next morning—good timing for the festivities!

Many people in Australia still think that aborigines cannot count because they do not use our system. But their sure feeling for number, which Spengler noted, enables them easily to adopt our symbols when introduced to them. An aboriginal child taught side by side with a white child will have no difficulty in doing his sums at the same rate of progress. One full-blood boy at a mission school in South Australia amazed his teacher, from the South Australian Education Department, by his ability in mental arithmetic. The teacher described the lad's facility as "fantastic" and far beyond that of any other child he had taught, either brown or white.

In 1934 the drop curtain designs at the Alice Springs Hall were done by an aboriginal full-blood lad. When I found him in a local store I asked him to draw something for me. On a thin piece of wrapping paper on the counter he drew with a piece of yellow ochre a perfect presentation of a tribal man, woman, and child on the move. No anatomist has ever faulted this drawing. But nobody ever encouraged him in his art; his job at Alice Springs was the cleaning of lavatory pans!

Without the aborigines the pastoral industry could not have developed. They handle horses and camels well, and can quickly become expert shearers. At Ernabella Mission they have done the shearing for many years; and in sheep country beyond the wild-dog fence, aboriginal families act as efficient shepherds of the flocks.

They have no difficulty in learning to drive and service cars when properly taught, and the story of their work at Daly Waters with aeroplanes is a fine example of co-operation between the two races. Before World War II Bill Pearce, a pioneer from England, was in charge of the aeroplane refuelling depot at Daly Waters in the Northern Territory. He had taken pains to understand and train bush natives whose intelligence he considered often surpassed that of the white man.

Aeroplanes from every part of the world were dealt with daily at the depot in record time, by Mr Pearce and five tribal trainees. The white man handled the mails, and the trained bush natives refuelled the planes while the passengers enjoyed a meal prepared by Mrs Pearce. It was a team with mutual confidence and implicit faith. Pearce's native employees were never exploited by him, never overdriven, never given inferior food, never worked when sick. All this was in marked contrast to conditions on some cattle stations run by some profit-making companies.

In his address to the A.N.Z.A.A.S. Conference, at Brisbane in 1951, Professor A. A. Abbie, anatomist and anthropologist, said:

> It is frequently claimed that the aborigines lack initiative, drive, and persistence. One might fairly inquire how much initiative, drive, and persistence the average white worker would display in the absence of supervision or, indeed, whether he would display as much persistence as the average aborigine, in say, tracking a wallaby. There

is a further statement that, while aboriginal school children can hold their own with white children, aborigines as a whole show little capacity for acquiring new ideas after the age of about fourteen years. It can scarcely be a coincidence that American Army intelligence tests in World War I gave an average I.Q. of fourteen years for white adults enlisting as recruits. And this figure appears to be applicable to whites generally.

In summarizing the chief points of his address Professor Abbie said:

There is no real evidence to support the belief that the average aborigine is mentally inferior to the average white.

A senior psychologist of the South Australian Education Department wrote to me:

From my observation and from tests done I would never dare to say that the aboriginal child is less intelligent than the white.

My own contact with aborigines in their tribal state and with those living in our civilization has convinced me that Australian aborigines are not as a race mentally inferior to the white race. When they are given respect, together with education and training for living in what for them is an alien culture, then the world will recognize the high degree of intelligence, versatility, and adaptability that is theirs.

That aborigines could be human beings with varying artistic gifts is a new conception for many Australians. Dancing is one of the artistic fields in which full-blood aborigines have always excelled, but recognition of this has nearly always come from outside Australia. Ted Shawn, world-famous American dancer, witnessed a native corroboree and saw a symbolic dance the following day. "I have seen some of the greatest dancers in the world, and this night I have seen them equalled," was his comment. He was even more impressed the following day. "Believe me when I say," he wrote to the New York *Herald Tribune,* "that at Delissaville I have seen primitive native dancers who, as expert choreographers and individual performers are equal to anything in the world." Of one dancer he said: "He is a superb artist. He could be taken right off his corroboree ground and transplanted on to the stage in New York and Covent Garden and be an immediate world sensation." Less than two years later this aboriginal died of pulmonary tuberculosis, unhonoured and unsung.

The aborigines are often consummate actors. Ealing Studios' film *Bitter Springs* required aborigines for extras. The South Australian Government arranged with the Commonwealth railways to transport 115 men, women, and children from Ooldea to Quorn, a two-day journey. They had to travel in two cattle vans and an obsolete railway carriage without lights, and with no sanitary convenience in the vans. It was known in advance that they would arrive in the dark on a cold night, yet when they arrived at Quorn in heavy rain no shelter had been erected for them. In damp clothes they were herded into a draughty wood and iron structure thirty feet by fifty feet until the morning, one blanket or ground sheet being all they had between them and the bitumen floor.

Tommy Trinder, who worked with these aborigines for weeks, said in Melbourne on his way to Britain that he had been told "Aborigines are the laziest creatures on earth—won't work, steal anything, and are completely untrustworthy." There was no trouble at all over their honesty; he had found them "quick, intelligent, natural-born actors with a great sense of humour and a lively curiosity about how things worked." "Aborigines," he said, "got a rotten deal," and should be educated to live as civilized people, or given better land for their reservations. It was admitted that the acting of the aborigines in *Bitter Springs* stole the show.

The next film in which aborigines appeared was *Kangaroo*, and again the Ooldea natives were brought down by the South Australian Aborigines Department, the men to be paid ninety shillings a week and the women fifty shillings. These wages angered the Secretary of Actors' Equity, Mr Hal Alexander, who accused the Department of "flagrant racial discrimination." But the Minister then in charge of native affairs referred to the enterprise as a "paid holiday." For he knew the amounts fixed to be far in excess of any previous earnings aborigines had received at Ooldea.

In June 1951 aborigines from North Queensland produced *Moomba* in the Princes Theatre, Melbourne. Everyone was excited, State Premiers, guest artists, and theatre-goers alike. The show was to tour Australia. Garnett Carroll, entrepreneur, and Daryl Lindsay, distinguished Australian artist, jointly advocated overseas showings. *"Moomba* has excited people," they said, "beyond anything we've known previously in the world of theatre. In *Moomba* there is something completely Australian. Its character, compounded of the purely aboriginal in literature, dancing, and singing, must be preserved in its entirety." . . . "It is something we must give the world before our native people die out." The producer, Miss Irene Mitchell, said "If we don't grab this chance with both hands, it will be a crime." But nothing happened; the aborigines were just sent back home.

In 1953 came the production of *Jedda,* with aboriginal stars Ngarla Kunoth and Robert Tudawali. Theirs was superb acting, and Tudawali has since filled several important dramatic roles.

Sculpture was another field in which an aboriginal was found to excel. Thirty years ago in Western Queensland a young tribal woman carried on her creative work "in between her station duties of cooking, and doing for her husband and children." Kalboori Young, as she was called, used two kinds of clay, which she had to search for. Using a fine flake of quartz, with deft fingers she set to work whenever she found the material.

The work was hailed by artists in Sydney as "work of creative genius. The objects are beautifully done in their primitive formalized style, and attain an emotional force and sincerity which twentieth-century artists have often sought to imitate." "There must be many Kalboori Youngs among our natives," said her sponsor, Mr R. H. Goddard; "why not give them the opportunity of establishing their artistic tendencies and develop a practical industry among the various groups scattered throughout Australia." But this appeal was ignored.

About the same time a full-blood Aranda tribesman was painting water-colours in the white man's style—pictures that were to bring wealth and fame for the first time to an aboriginal. I first met Namatjira in June 1934 at the Lutheran Mission, Hermannsburg, as he came in from the bush with a log of mulga. These logs provided him with slabs of wood on which he made drawings with heated fencing wire. He was then about thirty-two years old, and it was just two years before he began painting with water-colours.

In 1939 I had the honour to open Namatjira's first exhibition of water-colours in Adelaide at the Gallery of the Royal Society of Arts. In 1952 at the same gallery I opened a joint exhibition of the paintings of Namatjira and the Pareoultja brothers, Edwin and Otto, who with others were then doing interesting work.

In my opening remarks on this occasion I asked why it was that in less than twenty years there had been such an outpouring of paintings by full-blood aborigines in a style entirely new to them. Native art was conservative, controlled by tradition, and gave no outlet to the young men to create. They had to keep on copying tribal circles and lines. Traditional art was representational; aborigines tended to look down rather than across as we do. But in 1934 the Victorian artists, Battarbee and Gardner, set out on the veranda of the Hermannsburg Mission their paintings of the Aranda landscape.

For two days the aborigines sat in wonder; for the first time they were looking at their country as they had never seen it before, and in colour. Namatjira was particularly impressed, and asked Pastor Albrecht to buy painting material. This was done, but Namatjira failed to satisfy himself. When Rex Battarbee returned two years later Namatjira at once offered his services as camel-man in exchange for lessons in painting.

Touring with Battarbee for two months, he was given basic lessons only, but those two months of concentrated help set Namatjira on his feet as an artist—his own ability did the rest. Two years later, in 1938 in Melbourne, Battarbee arranged Namatjira's first exhibition of water-colours, and all forty-one paintings were sold. This record was maintained in successive exhibitions, and before he died he had sold paintings to the value of over £50,000.

The Sydney *Bulletin* in 1945 described Namatjira as:

> an aboriginal who could paint water-colours which beyond all dispute could immediately be compared without patronage with the standard paintings of the day. . . . And there is this too to be said: if an aboriginal can paint as well as the full-blooded Namatjira there's nothing the race can't accomplish.

Six years later, reviewing Bex Battarbee's book *Modern Australian Aboriginal Art,* the *Bulletin* said of Namatjira:

> An intense personal sensitivity shows in his work; a totally unexpected delicacy along with the warmth and strength. There have been water-colours of Namatjira's which one liked quite as well as Heysen's, and among the 21 reproductions in *Modern Australian Aboriginal Art* his right to stand equal with the leading white Australian water-colourists of the day is as clearly demonstrated as is his superiority over the other aborigines.

Yet when in 1962 the Federal Government arranged to have an exhibition of Australian paintings at the Tate Gallery in London not one by the famous aboriginal artist was included.

Namatjira was a guest in our home in Adelaide on the three occasions he came south. He expressed a wish to meet people of his race resident in Adelaide, and one evening a gathering was arranged by the Aborigines Advancement League, when he talked with the local aborigines.

During his next stay in Adelaide he visited the Millswood hostel for aboriginal girls, run by the same League. Here he gave great pleasure to the schoolgirl residents by meeting and talking with them. The Matron and Namatjira were relatives; they met again at my home. My wife and I will never forget the longing with which he regarded our little bush cottage in the hills one Saturday afternoon. He told us how much he would like to own such a little house; he had bought a town block in Alice Springs, fenced it ready to build, but was refused a transfer. "Now my wife and I have to camp in the bush," he said.

Quite apart from his art, Namatjira was an outstanding man. The first impression on meeting him was that here was a man of unusual dignity. He was highly intelligent, had deep sympathies, and possessed a wider knowledge of affairs than most people gave him credit for. And in congenial company he was full of fun. At breakfast one morning I read aloud from the daily paper a visiting anthropologist's belief that aborigines could withstand much greater degrees of cold than a white man. Chuckling with laughter, Namatjira said "That's funny; last night I had to pull up an extra blanket!"

He was devoted to his wife, and his first thought on arrival in Adelaide was always to send her a telegram.

He was neither awed by reporters, nor elated by the attention that came with his growing fame. Arriving at Adelaide railway station after his presentation to Her Majesty the Queen at Canberra, he was met by the Press. He was plied with questions, and many photographs were taken. One photographer said "I suppose, Mr Namatjira, you have been photographed in the past three weeks more than in all your life."

The full-blood man, towering above the Press-men, replied that photographs had been taken everywhere, but that back home in Alice Springs he would forget about them.

Full citizenship status became Namatjira's in recognition of his achievement as an artist, but he was reluctant to accept it. Perhaps he realized that it would be impossible for him to be loyal to conflicting laws, for he was by birth and training a tribal full-blood and as such had to share everything with his people. He was not only an artist; he was a fine character with high standards of loyalty to family and kin, and a greater sense of responsibility than those people in capital cities who introduced him to social sipping of alcohol. For in time he became fond of it and shared his new possession with his tribal kith and kin.

But their citizenship status was restricted; for them the drinking of alcohol was illegal, and Namatjira broke the white man's law in letting them have access to it. He was tried in court at Alice Springs and sentenced to six months' gaol, later reduced to three, to be served at the Haast Bluff section of the Papunya settlement two hundred miles west of Alice Springs.

Namatjira was a sensitive man; he brooded over his fate and never fully recovered from the indignity. He died, after a very short illness, on 8 August 1959.

In days to come Namatjira will be rated at his true worth: one of Australia's really memorable men—the outstanding sufferer in the aborigines' dilemma.

13

Sustenance ... Disease ... Shelter

"They can do with less food than we can."

"They won't live in houses."

ONE OF THE worst features of the contact between the advancing
white race and the dark race in Australia has been the lack
of food provided for the aborigines after their natural food has
been seriously diminished or lost to them. There is no doubt
that this has resulted in dangerous malnutrition for thousands of
aborigines throughout Australia. Malnutrition has been the
greatest long-standing damage inflicted by us, and the one least
acknowledged with shame.

For generations there has been an extraordinary conception
that aborigines can subsist and maintain health on much less food
than people of European stock. I have met with this idea even
on some of the missions. It has been very much more in evidence
on many cattle stations, where native workers have been given
food that was hopelessly inadequate for the maintenance of
strength. As for the dependants of workers—these had short
shrift. One of the grimmest scenes in my memory was the
sight, in 1935, of emaciated women and children clamouring
for the entrails from a bullock that had just been killed on a
cattle station.

In 1956 public concern was greatly roused by reports of
severe malnutrition in the Warburton Ranges area. A select
committee of the Western Australian Parliament had been
appointed to investigate the conditions there, and later its
chairman, W. Grayden, published a book describing by word
and photograph the pitiful condition of aborigines in this
drought-stricken area.

In the same year an A.N.A. pilot, J. Ferguson, when he was
surveying the Canning River basin in Western Australia, spotted

aborigines in a shocking condition. He brought back two of them. One was a boy about ten years of age but weighing only three stone and so weak that he had to be carried by the natives, themselves suffering from near-starvation. The other, a woman with an infected wound, was painfully thin. Such conditions were not confined to Western Australia; a year later the Director of Health in the Northern Territory, Dr R. C. Webb, told the Legislative Council that "for every thousand native children born, two hundred die in the first year of life," and he added "malnutrition was the main cause of death."

In the Northern Territory, until about 1940, Government rations for needy aborigines were utterly inadequate, as the official scale will show: "Not more than five lb. flour, one lb. sugar, and four oz. tea per week, and then only for the aged, infirm, and sick." Flour, tea, and sugar formed the basic ration for aborigines in all the States.

But in 1952 the Department of Health of the Commonwealth of Australia brought out a provisional ration scale "to help implement the 'cultural assimilation' declared by the Hon Paul Hasluck, Minister for Territories in 1951." This schedule was reviewed later, and ration scales for the feeding of aborigines were issued in 1957 for the guidance of missions, Government institutions, and cattle stations in the Northern Territory.

Table I is a basic scale for all women and non-working men. It is designed to provide approximately two thousand, eight hundred calories, plus all the nutrients in amounts recommended by recognized authorities.

Table II lists extra issues of certain foods for working men, children, and lactating mothers.

Table III lists foods which should be issued as required to kitchens, or wherever it is practicable to provide variety in the menus.

Table IV is a special scale for infants under fifteen months to whom other tables do not apply.

Table V gives a summary of the allowances made for groups of different ages and occupations.

The Federal Department of Health issued directions for the use of this scientific ration scale together with books of recipes. Unfortunately the Federal Government has no responsibility for aborigines outside the Northern Territory. If this scale could be enforced throughout Australia, malnutrition and deaths through lack of nutrition would soon be things of the past.

The Government settlements in the Northern Territory use these ration scales, but I know of only one mission in Australia that adopted them, and then only as a basis. The situation on cattle stations varies widely according to the outlook of the owner or of the manager in charge.

The very high death rate among aboriginal babies in the outskirts of white civilization has been due mainly to sub-nutrition or malnutrition, the result of underfeeding of mothers, inadequate medical attention, and an utter lack of supplementary feeding of infants. Lack of protein in all cases has been the main factor. Aboriginal mothers keep babies on the breast for at least two years, and often much longer, for the obvious reason that children without teeth cannot chew rough food. If the mothers do not get sufficient protein the baby suffers.

In an inland area the death rate among full-blood aboriginal babies and toddlers following epidemics of measles, influenza, and dysentery had been very high. Passing that way in 1957 I was asked to see three babies—dehydrated, flaccid, very thin, just whimpering weakly, and suffering from dysentery. Unless special protein feeding and vitamins could be given without delay death was inevitable. I asked that they be flown to Adelaide for admission to the Children's Hospital, but I was informed that because of heavy tourist traffic no room on a plane would be available for four days. "One of those three babies will die before that," was my comment. It did, and a second died at the Children's Hospital, in spite of the latest scientific approach and the most devoted care in attempts to save it. But the third child, although critically ill, responded in the hospital to high protein, vitamin-added diet.

Later I made an intensive investigation into the food supplied at that place, and also into how it was cooked and served. I found the food totally inadequate, and especially deficient in protein. I submitted a report and four months later—protein supplies having been sent up in the interval—the Commonwealth Health Ration Scale was adopted. Blood specimens were taken by two laboratory medical specialists, and the results, published in the *Medical Journal of Australia* a year later, confirmed my clinical findings. In the four years since then no deaths due to lack of nutrition have been noted in that area.

Lack of resistance to disease is inseparable from poor nutrition, and it is not surprising that aborigines have fallen easy prey to some of the diseases brought into the country. Dr Cecil Cook, in *The Epidemiology of Leprosy in Australia,* 1927, states that leprosy was brought to Australia in the nineteenth century by the importation of coloured labour from China and the Pacific Islands, it being previously unheard of among aborigines and early white settlers.

The year 1890 is given as the date when aborigines were first found to be affected in the Northern Territory, then part of South Australia, but "no steps were taken to protect the aboriginal tribes from their infected fellows until 1916 when the disease had already established itself in new areas."

In Western Australia the first reported case among aborigines was in 1908 at Roebourne on the north-west coast, an area where in pioneer days the original inhabitants had been more than once ruthlessly reduced. In Queensland there were cases among both Chinese and aborigines before 1890, but from 1890 to 1905 the majority of the sufferers were indentured Kanakas.

In May 1934 in an interview with the Minister for the Interior, the Hon J. A. Perkins, I urged that an investigation be made into the incidence of leprosy among aborigines of the Northern Territory—it was then said to be about one in two hundred and fifty. In February 1953 the Director-General of Health, Dr A. J. Metcalfe, rated leprosy the most serious medical problem in Northern Australia. The incidence among coastal aborigines was by then one in twenty, and in some places even worse. This was the highest anywhere in the world.

The Commonwealth Health Service of Darwin was responsible for control of the disease in the Northern Territory, but State Governments handled the matter in Western Australia and Queensland. A whole-hearted effort with modern drugs and adequate finance could check the spread of leprosy in one generation, and almost eradicate it in another. As Sir Leonard Rogers, well-known expert in this disease, said in London on 25 May 1954:

> The outlook for the unfortunate victims of leprosy has been immeasureably improved during the last 40 years and especially in the last decade. We may indeed envisage the possibility of the practical eradication of

the disease from our Empire within a very few decades if—and it is a very big if—the essential staff and funds are forthcoming.

But drugs alone are not enough; good food, good housing, a satisfying occupation, and the creation of hope materially help the cure. Contrary to popular belief leprosy is the least infectious of all infectious diseases.

Malaria is another disease that saps the vitality of aborigines in Northern Australia. To kill off mosquitoes in the north will be a major problem, but it could and should be done. In 1955 the World Health Organization decided on eradication of malaria through spraying of insecticides and administration of anti-malarial drugs. In less than five years eleven countries were clear of malaria. The same result could be achieved in Australia if money were voted for the purpose. According to latest reports, efforts in Queensland towards elimination of both leprosy and malaria have largely succeeded.

Hookworm disease takes heavy toll of the strength of aborigines in the tropics, for all the conditions conducive to its spread are present: warmth, moisture, and lack of sanitation. It can be eradicated only when methods of sanitation are taught and practised.

Tuberculosis, like leprosy, is an imported disease, but unlike it, it is not confined to the tropics. It is wide-spread among aborigines throughout Australia, and has in fact probably been the most decimating of all the imported diseases. I have seen tuberculous disease, acute and chronic, in many forms and at all ages. In the past ten years Federal and State Departments of Health have made surveys of aboriginal people, with appropriate treatment and the usual follow-up. Elimination of subnutrition by adequate feeding is a major factor in the control of tuberculosis among aborigines.

Yaws affects a great many of the race who are living more or less primitively. In the primary stage it shows on the skin; later, bones can be affected. I have seen great disfigurement of the face and severe debilitating infections of the body. In early days yaws was often wrongly reported as syphilis, and a great deal of unnecessary misunderstanding caused. In the treatment of yaws arsenical preparations have been superseded by penicillin. Concerted drives have eradicated the disease in other countries; and it should be tackled here under Federal control without delay.

Trachoma is a big problem in sub-tropical Australia where unhygienic conditions exist. It is easily spread and can cause blindness. Several ophthalmic surveys in the past seven years have been made for the Public Health Department of Western Australia. Aborigines chiefly have been found to be affected, but some white migrants coming in from southern Europe have had the disease in an active state. A long-acting sulphonamide is considered at present to be the most effective treatment.

Ulceration of the eye is another affection far too common in the interior. I have seen two cases where the cornea was destroyed and total blindness resulted.

Burns of the body are common because of the tribal practice of sleeping naked between two small fires. But the worst case of this kind I have seen was that of a young woman who had adopted clothing, had slept in her dress, and had been severely burned on back and chest by the smouldering cloth.

Infection of the ear—"running ear"—is prevalent among children in every camp.

A very painful condition seen among tribal people of the interior in winter is the deeply cracked thickened sole of the foot. The pain of this condition suffered by a person who has to be on the move must be excruciating.

The common venereal diseases contracted from the white man present no great problem among aborigines; syphilis is extremely rare, and gonorrhea is readily treated.

For the treatment and prevention of disease among aborigines, trained native personnel would be of the greatest value. It is unfortunate that the Australian Government in 1929 did not co-operate in the founding of the Central Medical School at Suva for the training of natives in the Western Pacific. From that medical centre, greatly enlarged in 1953, young native men of the Pacific have graduated every year in medicine, and young women in nursing. They have returned to their homes, and thereafter have been engaged in instructing local populations in hygiene, sanitation, and health. Several of them have achieved distinction in their profession. At the School of Tropical Medicine in Sydney, founded in 1930, one or two aborigines have been given instruction, and one is undergoing special training at the present time. But an annual output of aboriginal graduates to assist in the eradication of disease among the native people of Australia has not yet been envisaged. If the education of aborigines in the past had been brought up to the standard of the rest of the community there would have been no lack of available students of both sexes.

As aborigines are human beings like ourselves it is not surprising that they suffer from all the ills and peculiarities that flesh is heir to. There are many left-handed aborigines, and an occasional one has transposition of the viscera. These, and harelip, cleft palate, club foot, squint, and a cretin, I have encountered among tribal natives. There is the same range of common illnesses and the rarer diseases, but I cannot recall a case of cancer in tribal life.

Dr J. A. R. Miles, virologist, has stated in the *Medical Journal of Australia* that paralytic poliomyelitis is rare among Australian aborigines. Over ninety per cent of them five years old or more had neutralizing antibodies. Between the ages of three and four, fifty per cent had developed antibodies. I have seen two proven cases in female children under two years of age; both had paralysis of the legs.

Mental illness among aborigines is not unknown. In recent years a number of semi-tribal men working on stations have been certified in the interior as suffering from severe mental derangement. Under treatment in city mental hospitals many have recovered quickly. It may be that frustration in their environment and lack of understanding on the part of the management could have had something to do with the outbursts. Some aborigines, as in the case with some non-aboriginal people, have been born with less than average mental stability and are unable to cope with difficult situations. A trained psychiatrist in the Northern Territory Medical Service could do valuable work both in treatment and research.

Australia is fortunate in its Flying Doctor Services. A Federal Government Aerial Medical Service operates from Darwin for white people and aborigines alike in the tropics of the Territory. Always efficient, it was greatly improved early in 1959 by the introduction of direct radio-telephone and fast aeroplanes. There is a twenty-four-hour service, and the medical men of the Department of Health are rostered for the work. In addition to the call service, doctors in the Northern

Pitjantjatjara girl with perentie (goanna).

Drinking at a deep rock-hole, Musgrave Ranges.

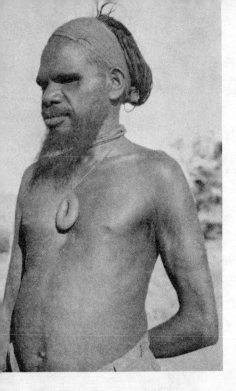

Blind medicine man of the Pitjantjatjara tribe.

Children digging for witchetty grubs, Musgrave Ranges.

Territory are allotted districts which they visit by aeroplane once a month. The population of the area served is predominantly aboriginal. In addition to this Government service there are two voluntary bodies.

The Royal Flying Doctor Service, the pioneer service, was started by the Rev John Flynn in connection with the Inland Mission of the Presbyterian Church of Australia in 1928. Through twelve bases linked by radio to cattle stations and missions it covers most of the inland, and in 1960 it extended its services to Tasmania. By means of an automatic alarm it is now possible to call a base at any hour of the day or night. This service is subsidized by the Federal Government.

There is also a radio Flying Doctor Service with its centre at Ceduna on the west coast of South Australia. This service is part of the Church Bush Aid Society of the Church of England. It covers a large area, and does splendid work. Both these voluntary medical organizations attend to aborigines as well as to white settlers.

A Flying Surgeon Service was inaugurated in Queensland on 1 July 1959 by the Minister of Health, Dr H. Noble, who realized the difficulties faced by medical men in far-back areas. The service is based on Longreach and the plane, now a twin-engined Cessna, carries in addition to the pilot, the surgeon, an anaesthetist, and a lot of equipment. More than twenty isolated towns, many having only one doctor, are visited regularly about once a month, and flights are made to emergencies at any time. The variety and extent of major surgery successfully performed by the surgeon in the first two years calls for the highest commendation. The service is for all in need.

This commentary on Flying Doctor Services would be incomplete without mention of the pioneer flying doctor of Australia, Dr Clyde Fenton. Fenton flew at night when needed, as well as by day, over uncharted country and in small single-engined planes in all weathers. For the six years before the second World War he operated from Katherine, situated two hundred miles south-east of Darwin; his practice covered 500,000 square miles, and when he retired he had flown 3,000 hours and covered 250,000 miles. He saved many a life, aboriginal as well as white, and was beloved of all. A man or woman's need was all that mattered to Clyde Fenton; the colour of the patient mattered not at all.

The aboriginal people of Australia can never live on equal terms with other Australians until they live in proper homes. To say, as is often done, that aborigines prefer not to live in houses is on a par with the old fable that aborigines could not be educated, and were fit only for the roughest manual labour, and under firm supervision. My experience, even with those who were tribal only a few years back, is that they do appreciate good housing, and the better the housing the more they rise to it if they have sympathetic guidance. It is entirely to their credit that they do not like earth or concrete-floored, unlined, galvanized iron huts without amenities, or water. Houses without bathroom, laundry, and sanitary facilities are better not built at all.

The housing of aborigines throughout Australia is very varied and far short of requirements. Educated part-aborigines in regular employment in metropolitan areas and in large country towns occupy the same type of home as white people, but too many aboriginal families live in substandard houses in the poorer quarters. In small country townships poor housing is the common lot of the native people, some of whom live in mere shanties of flattened petrol tins on the outskirts of the town. Filthy hovels only a few feet high are all too common on the fringes of our civilization.

All State Governments are seeking to build a few houses for aborigines in country towns, but the rate of progress is painfully slow, and nearly always protests are raised by some white residents. Sometimes a compromise is made, and inferior houses are built on the edge of a town. Two such Government-provided houses in an outback town known to me consist of four galvanized-iron huts, two of them divided into two compartments, and two into three. The entrance door is the only door; the floor is of concrete; the huts are unlined; light and air come from glass louvres. Opposite the entrance is a wood-stove. Water is not laid on, and there is no bathroom, wash-house, or toilet.

At a smaller township further north, the only houses provided are three galvanized-iron sheds open at one side with an earth floor nine feet by seven feet. On several visits to this township I found aborigines, who worked by day for white people, living in miserable humpies made of old rusty sheets of iron, forty-four gallon petrol drums, bags, and hessian gathered from the local dump—unsightly homes, but warmer in winter and cooler in summer than the open, specially-built sheds.

On some Government reserves a great many houses are far below acceptable standards, yet it is urged that people in reserves should become accustomed to modern amenities before moving into the general community. In these circumstances how can they do so?

Housing on Christian missions varies greatly: on some there is satisfactory housing, much of it built by the natives themselves under supervision, but on others no attempt at all has been made to provide this step in development. Few, if any, of the Churches could do the job without Government assistance.

Good housing and better living conditions are the most cherished desire of adult aborigines. They know that unless their children grow up with decent amenities they will leave school hopelessly handicapped in their struggle for recognition as equals with other Australians. A child who attempts to do his homework in a one-roomed or a two-roomed house, by candle or lamplight, without reading material, ruler or clock, in noisy chatter, and with parents unable to help, can never be expected to match his white schoolmates. And when the home in which he lives has neither bathroom nor toilet, the boy or girl goes out into the world socially as well as educationally handicapped.

But "fringe-dwellers" can change and improve their depressed mode of living if given proper help and encouragement. Mooroopna, a river township 115 miles north of Melbourne, provided the demonstration in 1958. Before that year aboriginal families were living on the banks of the Goulburn River in miserable earth-floor humpies which were flooded every winter. For children it was a hopeless environment—drunkenness was rife, and disease thrived in the squalor. Youngsters in rags could be seen scratching for morsels in the garbage tip. For years the Save the Children Fund distributed some food and milk. The senior constable of the district urged that the shanties be demolished, and several prominent citizens asked that decent houses be built for the aborigines.

There were immediate protests from some of the others that aborigines did not appreciate decent housing. But the Aborigines Welfare Board of Victoria, in conjunction with the Housing

Commission, built ten small houses of prefabricated slabs. Each house consisted of a large living room, three small bedrooms, bathroom with bath, copper, and a large sink. Lighting was by electricity, and there was a wood-stove.

The scheme was intended only as a half-way stage to accommodation more in line with the general standards of the white community. Rents have been paid regularly, furniture bought, good floor-covering installed by the people, and they have even bought sewing machines and refrigerators.

In less than a year there were well-kept gardens and vegetable plots. The children, clean and tidy, went to school, and the fathers, getting regular employment and wages, were able to provide adequate meals. Not one single person in the new housing area has been arrested for anything.

Four years later, at Dimboola, two hundred miles west of Melbourne, the Victorian Aborigines Welfare Board achieved a similar result, after overcoming the usual protests.

But there is one area in Australia at least where no housing programme of any kind has been started; that is the eastern goldfields of Western Australia. In 1961 at Kalgoorlie, the chief town of the goldfields, a meeting of residents protested to the Minister for Native Welfare, the Hon C. P. Perkins, against the building of houses for natives near the homes of white people. It was admitted this was the type of assimilation they desired for natives elsewhere, but Kalgoorlie was different!

The Minister gave an assurance that no homes for native people would be built west of Kalgoorlie without the full approval of local authorities and residents. He further expressed himself against native cottages being built on the Native Reserve. "The word would soon get around that Kalgoorlie had good shelter for natives, and they would come here in greater numbers." Must semi-tribal aborigines be driven back to desert land which they had left in search of greater security? If so where lies their future?

The plight of aborigines in the eastern goldfields is one of the saddest in Australia. For about thirty years semi-tribal aborigines from the desert country north-east of Laverton and Kalgoorlie have come into civilization in search of work; and they are still coming. Casual labour, often for only weeks at a time and at very low rates of pay, as station hands or as woodcutters, proved to be the best they could hope for. It was not uncommon for first-rate aboriginal workers to be employed for only three months out of twelve.

Few of these people had any idea of Federal Social Service Unemployment Relief, and although State relief was available the Commissioner of Native Welfare, in a direction to all Missions in the State 11 October 1956, ruled that: "In an attempt to maintain subsidy within our Departmental means I have decided not to subsidise adult natives under sixty years of age (according to records of this office) except those who are totally and permanently incapacitated." Under the conditions prevailing in the eastern goldfields decent living was beyond the reach of the majority of aborigines, and few would be able to pay rent even if houses were available. Humanity, however, demands that this local dilemma be resolved without further delay.

Viewing housing for aborigines in Australia as a whole in the light of increase of full-blood population and the very great increase of part-aborigines, there is no likelihood of anything like sufficient houses being provided in the near future. There is a constant shortage of houses in every State, and the white population invariably gets first preference.

14

Education ... Employment ... Citizenship

"They can't take education after fourteen years old."

"They're not worth a wage."

"They can't be trusted with citizenship."

PRIMARY EDUCATION AT State public schools is compulsory for aboriginal children living in the white community. Almost without exception these are part-white children. A few now attend technical or high schools, and a considerable number of these secondary students have had their primary education in Government settlement schools—segregated, of course, but sometimes under the control of the relevant State education department.

Part-white children on the fringe of small up-country townships are in a different category. Many of them are living in conditions that make cleanliness of body and clothing very nearly impossible, and when that is so they are precluded from attending the local State school. This group of children presents another problem—how to give education to children of parents who move from place to place in search of casual labour. Schooling is constantly interrupted, and learning negligible.

Aboriginal children at missions attend the mission school but few if any of these schools provide anything like full primary school requirements. Too often the building is unsuitable, staff is inadequate, and many of the teachers are untrained. But at missions where tribal or semi-tribal aborigines are first taught in the vernacular, where the teachers are fully trained and have an understanding of the people, good results are achieved.

In the Northern Territory the Federal Government in 1950-51 evolved a scheme for education of full-blood children on some cattle stations and on the new Government settlements of the Territory. The schools on these settlements are modern and well equipped, and the staff are trained teachers. But throughout Australia the number of aborigines, full-blood and even half-caste, growing up without any or with only a minimum of education is far too large, and very, very few get pre-school or after-school training.

It must now be recognized by all Governments that dark children are as much the responsibility of Education Departments as are white children, and whenever proximity allows, children of aboriginal blood should attend ordinary State schools rather than special schools such as exist on many Government settlements and missions. The mingling at lessons and in games is of the greatest value to white and dark children alike. A fine step would be the establishment of pre-school centres where small children of both races could become aware of new interests and joys arising from different cultures. In this way aboriginal children could begin school life with fewer social handicaps. But the actual fact is that in 1960 full-blood children and about half the part-white children were attending segregated schools.

In intelligence aboriginal children are in no way behind white children and, like children the world over, some are very bright, some dull, with the majority between the two extremes. But their educational progress is hampered by home conditions that do not have quietness for study, good lighting or ready reading material. Futhermore, the lack of stimulus from parents, themselves understandably dispirited by experience, and the baneful attitude of the majority of Australians to their race, sap them of incentive. When it is considered how recently education has been compulsory for them, and how great the handicaps they have had to face it is amazing that many have done so well.

At the tertiary stage the National Union of Australian University Students has provided scholarships for aborigines to study at Universities. And the Australian Colleges' Association has made provision for boarding aboriginal students at University Colleges when the need arises. So far very few aborigines have qualified for University training, and the number will remain small until they are convinced that there is a place for them in the economy of Australia after the long years of study.

Education is undoubtedly the main plank that enables aborigines to cross the gulf that exists between their culture and ours, and when it is fully extended to them some surprises are in store for us. Aborigines in the tribal state can speak the language on either side of their own country as well as their own, so it is not surprising that they are good linguists.

Sir Terence Murray, father of Gilbert Murray, O.M., was High Commissioner at an exhibition in Paris in the eighteen-sixties, and he took with him a full-blood aboriginal man. Visitors, especially Australians, were taken by surprise at the ease with which this man had learnt to speak French. My authority was the late Professor himself. Those of us who have had close contacts with tribal and semi-tribal aborigines know their facility in learning English. So there is obviously no place for broken or pidgin English in speaking to them. Only once did I make that mistake.

Looking anxiously for the track after we had left the last of the cattle stations on my first trip westwards, I saw two full-blood boundary-riders coming into sight, a man and woman on well-laden horses. As they approached, I asked the way in gibberish. Pointing with his hand the man replied "Quite near, just over there." What a fool I felt!

A full-blood aboriginal soldier on leave in London in the first World War sat by the fire reading a newspaper. An Englishman entering the reading-room was puzzled. "You read pape," he said, "very good, you savvy pape?"

The soldier politely replied, "Excuse me, sir, will you please speak in proper English if you wish to talk to me."

This aboriginal man is still living in New South Wales.

During the second World War the missions on islands north of Arnhem Land were visited by naval craft. At Goulburn Island an officer with some men came ashore. Lami Lami, an educated full-blood working on the beach with fellow tribesmen, was addressed by the officer in pidgin English. "Excuse me," said Lami with a smile when the officer had finished his halting discourse, "Are you one of the new Australians?"

At the Alice Springs Court 16 February 1951 a police prosecutor addressed an aboriginal full-blood witness: "You bin savvy this pfeller proper like? You bin savvy him all a same pfeller bin gib you bottle?"

"Yes, sir, I recognized the defendant immediately."

One further point. It is my own firm conviction that much of value in the culture and heritage of the aboriginal race has been lost to our nation because we have not educated aboriginal children in their own languages as well as teaching them ours. It has been the exception rather than the rule for any instruction at all to be given in the native tongue. My chief regret when I saw the otherwise excellent educational provision now made by the Federal Government in the Northern Territory was this fact. Not only was there no teaching in the mother tongue, but its use was actually discouraged in any educational or training programme.

U.N.E.S.C.O. has made it clear that the vernacular approach to education is the right one in every country, and W. H. Douglas, of Western Australia, has made a special study of the use of the vernacular in the education of the Australian aborigines. His findings were presented to the 1959 Conference of the Australian and New Zealand Association for the Advancement of Science. It is to be hoped that all of Australia's educational authorities will pay heed to this fundamental principle in the education of tribal aborigines.

Since the above was written the South Australian Government in December 1961, and the Queensland Government early in 1962, decided that in future the education of all aborigines in their States would be undertaken by the Education Departments.

Throughout Australia the aboriginal worker has received just remuneration for his labour only when he is sufficiently detribalized to be working side by side with the ordinary Australian working man, whose wages have been fixed by arbitration. The great majority of full-blood aborigines work on cattle stations, but everywhere they have been specifically excluded from the award rate.

Although the great pastoral properties could not have been developed without aboriginal labour, their working conditions have been almost uniformly bad. There has been the rare exception where a cattle owner has attempted to make some provision for the wives and families of his workers, members of the tribe whose country he has taken over. But on the great majority of cattle stations the aborigines have been forced to live as despised dependants, even the workers being often ill-fed as well as ill-paid.

Not only this, but little if any attempt has been made to introduce the station aborigines to the ordinary hygiene and sanitation of settled life or to provide even simple housing with washing facilities. There have been some stations where a colour bar was rigidly observed by day, but strangely enough it was frequently relaxed by night.

In an effort to correct these long-standing deplorable conditions, in so far as they occurred in the Northern Territory, the present Federal Government through the Minister for Territories, the Hon Paul Hasluck, drew up regulations 1959 No. 4 under the Wards Employment Ordinance 1953-59. These lay down conditions of employment, wages, hours of work, buildings to be provided, and so on. But these conditions have not been enforced, many pastoralists openly opposing the new regulations.

The minimum wage fixed for the pastoral industry was: for males two pounds a week, for females one pound a week, for minors under seventeen years sixteen shillings a week, at seventeen years twenty-four shillings a week, at eighteen, thirty-two shillings a week, at nineteen years full wage two pounds a week. In addition to the two pounds, fifteen shillings a week is payable as clothing allowance, and food and tobacco are to be provided. If an employee is married and living with his wife on the property then clothing and food for his wife and one child are to be provided. This wage, still far from adequate, is double the figure fixed by a conference between Native Welfare Officials and the Pastoralists' Association in January 1947, before which there was no wage.

But what of those who are unemployed and do not receive any wages? In the interior and north of Australia there is a great number of unemployed full-blood men, and the number is increasing. Some men are being trained at the Welfare Settlements in the Northern Territory and a few at missions, but in neither is all available manpower being employed. On cattle stations, because of the rapid introduction of mechanization, the number of aborigines being employed is decreasing.

When the Government of Australia recognized as a duty the full employment of all their people, it is certain that full-blood aborigines were not considered. But they must be considered, for to accept their idleness as inevitable and unimportant is to deny them human dignity. Yet the task ahead is fraught with difficulties. For there is little opportunity of learning a trade except in the capital cities and the larger towns, all in the South. To find employment for the aborigines in their own environment is the ideal, but the number of people in need of work is far greater than can be absorbed by present opportunities of employment in the inland. The solution to this problem must be regarded as one of Australia's most pressing responsibilities.

Employment of aborigines in Western Australia is very frankly discussed in the 1959 Annual Report of the Commissioner of Native Welfare. Lack of employment for aborigines was described as serious, and worst in the eastern goldfields already described by me. In the southern part of the State the report says:

> The native is usually first put off when reduction of work occurs. In Northern Districts, Broome and the Kimberleys; with few exceptions employers [pastoralists] are not attempting to raise the standard of their employees [aborigines]. . . . The town employer does not wish to pay much in wages nor provide food to the native employee; there would be none for his wife and children. This likewise applies to clothing issues. There are of course some employers who treat their employees reasonably well. . . . Machinery is needed to legally fix standards. . . . A small proportion of adult employable natives have proved unreliable in employment.

Continuing, the Report gives as a probable reason:

> . . . lack of education and lack of white contact in their early years. . . . The majority of natives, however, genuinely want work and the things that follow from regular employment, namely a home of their own and a more stable existence than the semi-nomadic one forced upon them by circumstances. But this Department cannot create employment. Field staff give every assistance possible in directing natives to jobs where such are known to be available but this represents a very few cases.

This factual statement is to be commended, but the conditions described are not peculiar to Western Australia. For casual labour and poor wages are the unhappy lot of the great majority of aborigines all over Australia. Even when work is fairly regular wages can be very poor.

In the latter part of 1961 new rates were gazetted for aboriginal workers on cattle stations in Queensland. This brought another demand from the Queensland Trades and Labour Council for aborigines to be paid on an equal basis with other workers, and to have the same general conditions of work. These new rates were still far below the rates paid to other workers under the State Station Hands' Award, but it was reported that the United Graziers' Association was to approach the Government in opposition to the new conditions.

The highest rate to be paid for an aboriginal station worker under the new 1961 regulations was to be ten pounds a week for drovers, plus food and accommodation, or two pounds five shillings in lieu of these two items. The Trades and Labour Council asked what kind of food and accommodation would be available for two pounds five shillings. An aboriginal farm labourer was to get eight pounds five shillings plus food and accommodation, whereas under the award the white general hand was paid fourteen pounds seventeen shillings and six pence and food and accommodation. Aboriginal workers were excluded from the Station Hands' Award and were thereby six pounds twelve shillings and sixpence a week the poorer. It must be noted, too, that the rates to be paid aborigines under the new regulations were in some cases reduced for those over forty-five years, even "if active." If "not active" at this age they were reduced still further. For example, general farm labourers aged twenty-one to forty-five years were to receive eight pounds five shillings; over forty-five years, if active, seven pounds ten shillings; over forty-five years if not active five pounds seven shillings and sixpence.

Is the presumed loss of activity so early in life due to poorer food and conditions than that enjoyed by white workers? And who is to judge whether there is decline of activity in the worker?

Discrimination was carried further. An aboriginal male cooking for Europeans was to receive eight pounds ten shillings a week, but if cooking for aboriginal workers was to get only seven pounds seven shillings and sixpence.

It is hard to believe that any attempt could be made to lower wages and conditions which were already so shocking, and even more difficult to understand how a Director of Native Affairs could respond to such a move. In March 1962, however, in *Queensland Country Life,* official organ of the United Graziers' Association of Queensland, the following statement appears:

> Following discussions between the Director of Native Affairs, Mr C. O'Leary, and the U.G.A. industrial officer, Mr P. A. Bartlett, the U.G.A. has been advised by the department that it is proposed to make certain changes to the wage rates payable to aborigines, and to other provisions of the Act.
>
> The existing daily rate, and the hourly rate of 8/- which was to have been paid to all aborigines, male or female, employed on a casual basis, are to be deleted, and will be replaced by an hourly rate for male casuals of 5/3, and a rate for females of 2/6 per hour. The existing minimum payment of 15/- which may be made to a casual, is to be replaced by a minimum engagement of four hours.
>
> The need for full adult wages to be paid to general farm labourers, houseboys, gardeners, etc., at the age of 18 years, is to be changed to 21 years of age.
>
> Where an employer does not provide food and accommodation, the Act presently requires that an additional £2/5/- shall be paid to the employee, and this amount is to be reduced to 25/-. This latter amount is also to be used for calculation purposes in connection with annual leave or where overtime is payable.
>
> It is not yet known from what date these changes will become effective, but the department has indicated that implementation will be as early as possible.

Surely this agreement reaches the rock-bottom of meanness!

It is a sad commentary that the sphere where aborigines' work has been best organized and most appreciated has been in the nation's war effort. But here again only when they were members of regular fighting forces were they adequately paid. The following is an extract from the Report on Administration of the Northern Territory for the year 1945-46— Appendix C.

> During the war years [World War II] approximately one thousand aboriginals were employed by the Armed Services on work about camps and on general labouring work. The duty performed by natives was excellent and resulted in the release of an equal number of enlisted men for fighting service. Separate camps were established for natives and they and their dependants were maintained as part of the remuneration paid. The actual cash payment amounted to only tenpence per head per day.

It was alleged by some that the food supplied to the labour gangs was inadequate for health and strength, and an investigation was made by a major of the Royal Australian Army Medical Corps. His report stated that the diet for natives employed by the Army "falls far short of minimum requirements and must bring about lowered resistance to infection which is what has been actually found to occur. In so far as this group of natives is concerned the solution is simple—they work at least as hard as Army personnel, they should be fed on standard Army rations."

That they worked "at least as hard as Army personnel" is confirmed by a report by Sergeant Victor Hall on their work on saw benches. Six aborigines sawed twenty tons of wood a day, but before they were employed (at tenpence a day) six white army personnel sawed only six tons a day.

Tribal full-bloods in the northern coastal belt proved invaluable in tracking lost airmen, wrecked seamen, and enemy personnel. A member of the R.A.A.F., Mr Lindsay Bacon, in a revealing statement to the *Sydney Morning Herald,* 28 November 1942 wrote:

> Up here at one particular cattle station in the far north of Australia we have the good fortune to be camped near a tribe of blacks. This tribe is completely uncivilized, having had practically no contact with Europeans. Down South one hears tales of the decadence and lack of intelligence of the Australian aborigines, but I can assure you that such a conception is

entirely false. I've never seen more virile, energetic and well-built specimens than the young men of this tribe. These natives are extremely friendly and very willing workers. As a result of this we use them for work about the place and pay them what, by our standard, would be a ridiculous amount, but to them is a marvellous wage. For example, pay for a full day's work is an inch cube of special native tobacco and two handfuls of flour. The natives love our bully beef, and in exchange for a small tin of meat they will bring in a wallaby, five or six geese, or else a few choice fish.

Comment is unnecessary.

In the Navy aborigines were employed as deck hands, and as pilots on ships in northern waters.

In addition to war work in Australia many aborigines served overseas in the Navy, the Army, and the Air Force in the 1939-45 war. One man rose to be a Captain in the Army; he and others served in Korea.

Reports such as these give the lie to statements so glibly made by people of fixed prejudice: "The abos are too lazy to stick to a job; they're not worth a wage." Aborigines work steadily in their tribal state to provide subsistence for themselves and families. But they are not alone in requiring proper incentive to work for others, nor alone in working better under good conditions.

What conditions have we provided for them, and what incentives?

The following list gives a rough estimate of the number of aborigines under special legislation in the different parts of Australia in 1960.

	Full-Bloods	Mixed-Bloods
Western Australia	10,800	8,100
South Australia	2,500	3,500
Victoria	0	0
New South Wales	235	13,360
Queensland	10,284	7,920
Northern Territory	17,112	0

These figures of course do not represent the total number of aborigines in Australia.

In Victoria there are very few full-bloods, but several thousands of mixed-blood people, all enjoying full citizenship. In the Northern Territory people of mixed blood are full citizens and they number about two thousand. In the Australian community there are thousands of people with some aboriginal blood included in the white population. This is especially so in the older States.

According to K. H. Bailey, Solicitor-General,

> All persons born in Australia are Australian citizens and British subjects by the operation of the Nationality and Citizenship Act. All full-blood aboriginals and all persons of mixed blood born in Australia are therefore Australian citizens and British subjects.

But the sovereignty of the States with respect to aborigines within their borders gives State Governments the right to restrict their State citizenship, as the following survey will show.

The *Sunday Times,* of 13 July 1958 reported that in Western Australia the Commissioner of Native Welfare, Mr S. G. Middleton, declared that "the most basic and urgent need of natives is restoration to them of their rights and privileges as citizens of our country." Yet he has to administer an Act that classifies all people of half or more aboriginal blood as aborigines under the Aborigines Act, and so are denied citizenship. The right to vote at West Australian elections is restricted to aborigines entitled to honourable discharge from the Services and to those who hold Citizenship Rights Certificates.

A Certificate of Citizenship implies that the holder has the same rights and privileges and the same responsibilities and obligations as a white person, but the certificate can be revoked. Relatively few aborigines have this precarious citizenship—thirty-three full-bloods and 1,550 mixed-bloods, plus their seven hundred and sixty children. In Western Australia education of aborigines is compulsory, and is under the State Education Department. Since 1955 there have been no restrictions in employment, wages, property, marriage, or in movement, but it is an offence for aborigines to be in possession of or to drink alcohol.

In South Australia everyone of any aboriginal blood, no matter how advanced in culture or training, is legally subject to the control of the Aborigines Act, and the status of full

The full-blood children who were refused admission to Elliot
School, N.T.

A group of tribal young folk from Ernabella to see the Queen in Adelaide.

citizen can be got only by exemption from the Act. An uncond tional and irrevocable exemption is provided for in the Act, but exemptions now are nearly always "limited" for a period of three years, during which time the applicant must satisfy the Aborigines Board that "character, standard of intelligence or development" are such as to justify the continuance of the exemption.

By many aboriginal people this process is considered a great indignity, and they refuse to apply for exemption, believing that citizenship in their own country is their birthright. In South Australia aborigines suffer no restriction in education, employment, wages, marriage, movement from place to place, or the franchise. But it is an offence for aborigines to drink alcohol or be in possession of it. There are other disabilities: the property and moneys of aborigines can be controlled, anyone can be sent to a Government Reserve and kept there, and "the Board shall be the legal guardian of every aboriginal child, notwithstanding that any child has a parent or other relative living, until such a child attains the age of twenty-one years." (As is mentioned on page 163, a new Act is being prepared.)

In Victoria as already stated all people of aboriginal blood are full citizens.

In New South Wales full-blood and half-caste aborigines are under an Aborigines Act, and such people have to apply for an exemption certificate to achieve citizenship status. It can be revoked. It is illegal in New South Wales for aborigines to drink alcohol, but they suffer no restriction in education, employment, marriage, franchise, or movement.

In Queensland all people with more than fifty per cent aboriginal blood, and half-castes declared by a Court to be in need of protection, are under the control of the Aborigines Act. In Queensland people with more than fifty per cent native blood are ineligible to vote, marriage is forbidden without the consent of the Director of Native Affairs, terms of employment and rates of wages are fixed by the Director and without his permission aborigines cannot move from one district to another.

Only pocket money out of wages is paid to the native employee, the remainder going into a savings bank account in his name. The money is held in trust, and even when a native becomes a citizen his money is still held until such time as may be determined by the Director. This hardly smacks of citizenship, nor does the fact that exemptions can be revoked. The amount of wage-money belonging to aborigines and held in trust on 30 June 1960 was £869,311/11/4 but "no aboriginal is precluded from operating on his Savings Bank Account for his immediate needs."

When an employer pays the aboriginal's wages into the Trust Fund it is taxed two-and-a-half per cent to ten per cent for the Aboriginal Welfare Fund (Regulation 6). And the Native Affairs Department may draw on the Welfare Fund "for the general benefits of Aboriginals" (Regulation 11).

The Education Department until 1962 had no control over schools specifically for aborigines. The Director of Native Affairs is the legal guardian or every aboriginal child under the age of twenty-one years, notwithstanding that parents or relatives of the child are living. Property of aborigines is under the control of the local protector—usually the policeman—who, subject to the approval of the Director, may sell or dispose of any property of an aboriginal, whether real or personal. It is an offence for aborigines to be in possession of or to drink alcohol.

In the Northern Territory, which is the responsibility of the Federal Government, full-blood aborigines with eighty-eight exceptions come under the Welfare Ordinance as wards, while part-aborigines, with the exception of any judged to be in need of care and assistance, have full citizen rights. Wards cannot vote, and permission is required for marriage. Employment of wards is regulated and is of two kinds, (a) apprenticeships; (b) training on the job. Wages are fixed (see the chapter on wages), and in part are paid into a trust fund, but the amount to his credit is paid over when the ward becomes a citizen. Wards cannot own property, nor are they free to move from place to place without permission. It is an offence for a ward to be in possession of or to drink alcohol.

The foregoing is the citizenship dilemma of the aborigines in the different parts of the Commonwealth of Australia. The dilemma must be resolved, and to me it is clear that everyone born in Australia should be eligible for all the privileges and protections of the law. No person should be free from responsibilities or denied privileges on the ground of race. The great majority of part-white aboriginal people living in the white community but still under the Aborigines Acts are earning and paying taxes under the same system as the rest of us. Their children are compulsorily educated, as are ours. To deny full State citizenship to such British subjects and Australian citizens is not only unjust, it is absurd.

It is often said that tribal and semi-tribal aborigines would not know what to do with citizenship. They need not, at that stage of their development, know what to do with citizenship, but when in due course they are ready for it the right is there for them to use. For some years they will need the guidance and encouragement of Government Welfare Officers in matters of health and hygiene, housing, education, and employment. Thereafter persons deemed unfit to assume responsibility, or in need of protection, should be aided under legal provisions pertaining to the whole nation.

On 31 October 1962, the South Australian Parliament passed an Aborigines Affairs Bill with the intention of abolishing all restrictions and restraints on people of aboriginal blood except primitive full-bloods. But it failed to remove the restriction on alcohol, except in areas which may be declared.

This limitation of freedom was presumably protective in aim. It is therefore all the harder to understand why the new Bill eliminates all special protection for aboriginal women on the edge of our civilization against sexual interference by irresponsible white men. Even alcohol has not been more devastating to the aboriginal race than the immoral use of their womenfolk

15

Social And Economic Development

"Missions spoil the Niggers."

"You'll never make them understand trade."

MISSIONARY EFFORT ON behalf of aborigines has never been able to claim the support of the whole Christian Church, and interest in overseas missions has always made a much stronger appeal. The belief that aborigines were a dying race, were not educable, were devoid of moral sense, and hardly to be regarded in terms of the Kingdom of God explains the fact that money and efforts planned on their behalf were sometimes diverted to other purposes.

But even in the nineteenth century, and since, there have been people who have made personal sacrifice in leaving the amenities of civilization and living among tribal aborigines in an effort to advance their welfare. And these missionaries have been loyally supported by the few in every Church.

Missions can justly claim to have been the pioneers in welfare work among aborigines, and they still make a valuable contribution in that field. Many mistakes have been made in the past, one of the main errors being an almost fanatical belief on the part of some missions that the aborigines should be turned as quickly as possible from their own ways to ours. As late as 1947 a defence of this attitude was made in the Press by a well-educated missionary.

But it must be remembered that but for the self-sacrifice of missionaries aborigines would be in a much worse position today than they are. Take, for instance, the Aranda people of the centre of Australia. The Eastern Arandas, unprotected by any mission, soon disappeared as a tribal group before the advancing cattle industry and the north-south railway line. But the Western Arandas were held and protected by the Lutheran

164

Hermannsburg Mission founded in 1877. And today there survives a thriving community—the home of the well-known aboriginal artists.

All the major denominations but one have missions to aborigines in Australia, and there are undenominational "faith missions." Some missions are in tribal territory, some among semi-tribal people, some among part-aborigines on the edge of white civilization. Others cater only for half-caste children whose fathers have left them. Some missions are well run, some are not, some stress a denominational angle, others teach mainly by example.

The hardest thing for the aborigines to reconcile is the Christian teaching of loving and sharing with the acquisitiveness that the white man shows. The missionary, even though his living conditions may be hard and simple by western standards, yet has individual possessions and comforts far beyond those enjoyed by the aborigines he is serving. As the aborigines have been trained since childhood to share all good things with others they must often be deeply perplexed by this apparent inconsistency.

All missions aim at inducing the aborigines to adopt the Christian faith, and some are not interested in anything else. I am firmly opposed to anything savouring of compulsion in religion. I have visited missions on islands north of Arnhem Land, on Arnhem Land itself, missions in the heart of Australia, and in the south. These visits have convinced me that the true way to win aborigines to a Christian way of life is for missionaries themselves to live Christ-like lives, and to leave the aborigines to make the change when they are convinced that the new way is better than the beliefs that previously sustained them.

Only the finest people should become missionaries, and all of them should be trained in a specific job. One of the reasons why aborigines were said in the past to be of low mentality was that many of the people who went to teach them were lacking in human understanding, and in intelligence, were poorly educated, and untrained in any skill or calling.

I have sometimes been asked to give a medical certificate of fitness to people offering for missionary work. On more than one occasion, when my inquiry revealed that no training in teaching, nursing, or other skill had been done, I was met with the assurance that this lack was of no importance because "where God calls He provides." I am convinced that the best possible training should be an adjunct to the strong Christian faith essential for the missionary's difficult task, and such training is now insisted on by Church Mission Boards.

Every mission that is so distant from the settled community that its children cannot attend a State school should have a well-planned and well-equipped school building, with trained teachers seconded from the Education Department if necessary, without any loss of promotion, superannuation, or salary. The school should be regularly inspected by the State Education Department, and full primary education demanded.

If a mission is catering for aborigines who still speak their tribal tongue, the people should be taught and made literate in their own language before advancing to literacy in a foreign tongue—in this case English. It has been proved everywhere that this is the surest way for aboriginal people to acquire a sound knowledge of any language that is not their mother tongue.

Vocational training is most important, with employment to follow. Workers should be paid an adequate weekly wage to enable them to buy their food and other necessities, the aim being to preserve their independence and in the process learn the use of money. One of the problems of outback Australia today is the great number of able-bodied full-blood young aborigines for whom work is not being provided, or provided only at a miserable wage. Idleness in the bush, as in the city, breeds discontent and mischief.

Missions to tribal and semi-tribal natives should have on the staff a man capable of giving industrial training, another versed in sheep or cattle work, and a woman trained to give instruction in domestic arts and craft work. With entry into our way of life in view, adequate training in housewifery for women seems to me of great importance, and for men some training in simple repairs and maintenance.

Every mission has, of course, a church building as its central feature, and it is usually well adapted to the climatic conditions prevailing. Spiritual teaching should always be given in the native tongue where it is still the everyday language of the people. A necessity is a small, modern, well-equipped hospital under the control of a Sister trained in general nursing, in midwifery, and, if possible, in child welfare.

Housing is another factor in the advancement of aborigines. The wiltja or wurlie made of stout bush timber with spinifex thatching provides shelter, and warmth comes from a small fire of hot embers. But when aborigines have lived for some years at a mission, and have had experience of the homes of the white staff, they very naturally begin to express a wish for a house. Material should be provided and the men trained to build their own homes. Provision of water for each house is an essential in the adoption of a settled life. At one mission that has been in existence for twenty-five years—a generation—the white staff have good homes, whereas the aborigines still live in tribal fashion in wurlies.

The most potent criticism of missionary work is the difference in the presentation of the Gospel by different missions. Why should the Gospel of Jesus be put forward with so many denominational variations?

Missions, on their part, have a valid complaint—they never have security of tenure. If pastoralists pester politicians for good land that happens to be part of a mission, or if metals should be found on the property of a mission, Governments can exert pressure. Quite recently the Queensland Government entered into a legislative agreement with a rich mining company, Comalco.

"Comalco" stands for Commonwealth Aluminium Corporation Pty. Ltd. formed by Consolidated Zinc in Queensland in December 1956. In November 1960 Kaiser Aluminium and Chemical Corporation of Oakland, California, became a joint equal partner. By mid-1966 an expenditure of about £A.130 million is envisaged in an alumina extractor plant at Weipa, the construction of a new shipping channel and port facilities, and a new township to house 2,500 personnel. By 1970 the white population is expected to be at least 1,000 more. All this is to happen in what was the native village in Weipa Reserve.

This agreement gave the company permission to extract minerals from two huge mission reserves—Weipa and Mapoon —the area leased extending to about two thousand five hundred square miles, on which stood two mission native villages.

In the concession legislation the rights of the natives were not dealt with, nor was the existence of aborigines even mentioned. The people of both these Presbyterian Missions are to be moved. The aborigines from Weipa will be housed in a new modern village to be built by, and at the expense of, the mining company. The site of the new village is to be distant by water three miles from the mining operations. A launch will enable aboriginal men to get to work, but strict supervision will be necessary to prevent men from the mining camp visiting the aboriginal village.

The aborigines at Mapoon are also to be moved, but this was under discussion before the coming of Comalco. The seventy-year-old mission required rebuilding, which would have entailed great cost, and the site was not considered suitable for development. The Queensland Church consulted the people, who were unanimous against moving, despite strong advice to leave. Later the Government made it clear to the Mapoon aborigines that they were expected to go to a Government settlement at Bamaga in the vicinity of Cape York. In the Bamaga area there were already five hundred Torres Strait Islanders, and more than two hundred full-blood aborigines. The new Mapoon will not be a Church mission as in the past; it will be controlled by the Queensland Department of Native Affairs, although a Chaplain is expected to be in residence. There are changed days ahead for both the Weipa and the Mapoon aborigines.

The whole tenor of aboriginal mission work is changing. The Superintendent of a mission today, in addition to being a Christian example, must have sufficient training in anthropology to enable him to understand the heritage of the people he serves and their pride in it. There is a strong case for the application of Social Anthropology to missions.

Still another change is coming. Few if any of the churches have enough money for the full-scale development of aborigines that is now required, and large Government subsidies are proving necessary. From now on Governments are likely to be increasingly responsible for the material side of mission welfare work, but missionaries will continue to provide moral and spiritual guidance. Strengthening of character is as important as training of the mind and hand; indeed, it is of greater importance if the difficult adjustment to our way of life is to be successfully made.

But whatever be the ultimate change it must never be forgotten that when Governments were indifferent or repressive to the aboriginal race, it was the Christian Church that provided material as well as spiritual aid. Most important of all—every member of the Christian Church must recognize his or her responsibility for the welfare and advancement of the aborigines throughout Australia. The Christian community must not confine its concern to the relatively few aborigines living on missions.

Aborigines living on cattle stations have been largely ignored as a field of Christian service. In my experience only the Lutheran Pastors Albrecht, father and son, have sought to meet this need.

It is inevitable that the aborigines should have great difficulty in moving from their tribal economy to ours. No better aid has been found to bridge this gulf than the co-operative.

The South Pacific Commission, in Technical Paper No. 123, had this to say:

> In an underdeveloped community ignorant of either economic or political organization in the modern sense, harnessing of the community spirit is about the only means available to development by stimulation as opposed to imposition.
> The peculiar ability of a co-operative to reconcile economic advantage to the individual with the interests of the community as a whole renders it especially suitable for such a community.
> The social aspects of co-operation are far-reaching. Co-operatives, by involving their own members in management problems, create experience for many people, thus giving better opportunities to develop talent and skills which otherwise might not have been reached.
> The formation and effective operation of co-operatives present many difficulties . . . to overcome which a significant measure of government support and skilled supervision is necessary.

What Papua and New Guinea have done—co-operators there in just over six years have accumulated capital of £400,000—Australia can do if the Governments give encouragement and help and if trained instructors are made available. But some State Governments and some mission executives have shown no liking for co-operatives.

The Pindan Proprietary Group came into being in the north-west of Western Australia in 1946. In 1945 many aboriginal men with their families had walked off cattle stations in the Kimberleys where they were getting rations and a few shillings a week. Nearly all of them lived on the banks of creeks, without housing or amenities of any kind. These people, under the guidance and stimulation of a white man—Don McLeod—formed the Pindan co-operative to enable them to achieve independent living. The base or supply camp of the group is two miles from Port Hedland, and there are another seven camps spread over the surrounding country.

At each camp there are well-constructed huts with lavatories, washrooms, and well-equipped laundries. The dogs, always an important part of aboriginal life, are tied up at some distance from the camps. The camps are well kept, the people self-respecting, and at ease. Surface mining, pearl fishing, and the collection of buffel grass are the principal occupations. The camps are controlled by committees to which both men and women are elected. These committees maintain an absolute ban on violence, and they do not allow alcohol in the camps. This co-operative is now entirely under the control of aborigines.

A Christian Community Co-operative Ltd. has been started by the Australian Board of Missions, Church of England. Its Director, the Rev W. A. Clint, is a man of wide experience in the co-operative movement. In Queensland, at the Lockhart River Mission on the east coast of Cape York Peninsula, Father Clint started a producers' co-operative which is run entirely by 150 aborigines as a profit-sharing scheme. Trochus fishing was the main activity, and the people's response to the co-operative idea soon resulted in their becoming an independent, self-respecting community. They faced difficulties with the fall in value of trochus shell, and this illustrates the fact that a producer co-operative needs several major activities, as any product may fall in value.

At Cabbage Tree Island, New South Wales, a co-operative was started in 1960 with an initial capital of £250, and a membership of twenty-one people. In less than a year there were forty members. It is now registered in New South Wales as a Rural Co-operative Society. Sugar-cane was planted and will be ready for harvest in 1963, and other crops are being planted. The New South Wales Government has guaranteed a loan of £3,000 through the Commonwealth Bank, to enable the co-operative to establish a "Wage Loan Pool"; this will help in giving the aborigines economic security by paying wages until the crops are harvested. Adult education co-operative school classes are held regularly; a post office conducts all business, including child endowment and pension payments.

At Condobolin, New South Wales, a co-operative was formed in 1962. It is registered as a Community Advancement Co-operative Society. As a first project they are building their own recreation hall and intend to develop market gardening. The New South Wales Government Aborigines Welfare Board has made a grant of £350 towards this effort, and the people themselves up to May 1962, had raised over £150. Adult education classes are held here, and also at Murrum Bridge, N.S.W., where a Rural Co-operative Society is to be formed when the people are ready.

Moa Island Co-operative Society, Torres Strait Island, is trying hard in fishing, but has met with many difficulties, in spite of which the Directors are showing steady persistence.

Tranby Co-operative Centre in Sydney—"training ground of the Co-operative Movement in Australia for Australian Aborigines and Pacific Islanders"—has been granted £5,000 by the N.S.W. Government for more accommodation and lecture rooms. It is hoped to make Tranby a Residential College for teaching the principles and practice of co-operation.

In South Australia a consumer co-operative at Point Pearce Government settlement was begun in November 1956 by the then headmaster of the local State school, Mr Ron Neilson. He taught interested aborigines the principles and details of co-operative trading. They built a store, and within a few months an aboriginal committee assumed control. Within two years they had a turnover of £12,000.

There is no doubt that if co-operative efforts received support and encouragement from their respective Governments, success would be assured and others would follow.

Established as the aborigines are in the age-long tribal custom of sharing, and faced with the difficulty of entering our acquisitive, competitive society, there can be no better introduction for them than the co-operative. Here they are able to learn our modes of producing and consuming without losing their own inherent principle of sharing.

16

Protective Policies

"Natives can't be allowed to hinder progress."

"Show them who's master."

FOLLOWING THE PERIOD of extermination which occurred in the nineteenth century while the incoming race pushed inland from the coast came the days of reserves. Early in the twentieth century large tracts of land removed from civilization were set aside to allow tribal aborigines to lead their traditional existence of hunting game and gathering food. The land in these reserves had belonged to the tribes in early times, and they had lived there for thousands of years. But the reserves have never been recognized as inviolable, and whenever the land has been considered of value to the white man the aborigines have found themselves pushed aside without title or tenure.

Two years after gold was found on the Tennant Creek aboriginal reserve in 1931, the Warramunga tribe was expelled from its tribal country to a newly created reserve, with little water, poor game, and no tribal significance, ten miles east of Tennant Creek. In 1946 they were moved to another waterless area, Phillips Creek, thirty miles north of Tennant Creek. After a generation of being moved from one place to another, the remnant was finally transported to the modern settlement at Warrabri in 1956.

In April 1936 the Western Australian Government granted a permit to the Border Gold Reefs Ltd., of Sydney, to enter the western section of the Central Aborigines Reserve to inspect what was claimed to be Lasseter's gold reef. I protested against this breach of the reserve. Four months later a Government geologist, Mr H. A. Ellis, after an investigation, charged the company with making fraudulent claims. But in those four months the reserve was violated.

172

In 1951, minerals were found in the Arnhem Land Reserve in which Church of England and Methodist missions were at work on behalf of tribal aborigines. The following year the Director of Native Welfare, Mr F. H. Moy, in the Legislative Council of the Northern Territory introduced a Bill to legalize mining operations in the Arnhem Land Reserve. In 1958 a mining lease was granted to Reynolds of U.S.A. in north-east Arnhem Land, and it was soon encircled by another mining lease granted to an Australian company, Duval Holdings. In southern Arnhem Land the Zinc Corporation took an option over a load of silver lead. Lessees of areas on Northern Territory aboriginal reserves have to pay a royalty of 2½% of value of minerals recovered to a Wards (Benefits from Mining) Trust Fund.

Bauxite was found in 1956 in quantity in Cape York Peninsula, and, as mentioned in the previous chapter, the Queensland Government by legislative process leased to Comalco, the powerful mining company, huge areas of native reserves. The deal fixed royalties to the Queensland Government, but legislation made no provision for the aborigines and their rights.

But Comalco is not the only group interested in bauxite in Cape York Peninsula. Alcan, Aluminium of Canada, has secured large leases not far removed from the Consolidated Zinc-Kaiser deposit at Weipa. One can safely say that the end of these aboriginal reserves in Cape York Peninsula is in sight.

Probably better known is the historic case of the Great Central Aborigines Reserve in the heart of the continent. The Central Reserve, roughly sixty-five thousand square miles in extent, was made up of more or less equal portions from the Northern Territory, South Australia, and Western Australia created in 1920, 1921, and 1937 respectively. For thousands of years men, women, and children had lived in the vicinity of the numerous mountain ranges in the reserve, roaming in search of food from place to place within their allotted territory. Water, native game, and vegetable food were all found along or near the ranges. But away from the good land adjoining the mountains the reserve is a desert of sand, spinifex, and desert oak. That it was a hard life calling for physical fitness and keen intelligence I saw in my two trips through the Reserve.

This reserve is now a rocket range. Graded roads now cross the old Reserve; mining has taken place along the ranges that were the vital highways of the tribal people, and a meteorological station—Giles Observatory—has been built within five miles of one of the chief meeting grounds of the tribes, Sladen Waters, a permanent water soak.

In the past nothing was ever done for the aborigines of the reserve even in times of drought, but by contrast the white men of the observatory have air-conditioning, an air-strip, and a well-made road to the north-south railway five hundred miles away.

The tribal life of the aborigines in their home country is in the process of being destroyed. They are losing cohesion, and in a generation or two, unless something is done at once, they will have ceased to exist except as oddments here and there without any hold on life.

In May 1956 at the Assembly of the Presbyterian Church in South Australia I stated that a new approach must be made to the tribal aborigines in the Central Reserve; that a settlement of some kind should be established in the South Australian part of the reserve to help the natives face the new conditions forced upon them. Visits during the winters of 1957 and 1958 to that part of the reserve under the control of the Presbyterian Church of Australia led me to advocate the introduction of a cattle industry there.

This was subsequently investigated, and a major plan evolved by the Board of Missions was subsidized by the South Australian Government. The South Australian Government did more than this, for in 1961 it laid the foundation of a project to train aborigines in the cattle industry, eighty miles deeper in the reserve. The Federal Government had already established a settlement, its section of the reserve, Papunya, on progressive lines to encourage the tribal people in its section of the reserve to adopt the "western" way of living.

No one can deny that changes brought about by Governments and commercial enterprises in the Central Reserve in recent years have disturbed the balance with nature achieved by the aborigines of Australia over thousands of years, and that further disturbance is certain. The days of food-gathering and hunting are nearly over, and as we are the cause of the drastic change it is our plain duty to introduce these first Australians to a more settled existence in which they can be as self-reliant and self-supporting as they were in earlier days.

Reviewing what has happened to aboriginal reserves in different parts of Australia over the past thirty years one is forced to ask whether "the gradual but inexorable process by which the people were dispossessed of their heritage" is to continue. We have confiscated without any thought of recompense and without shame the total land of the aborigines. Will the day ever come when land in Australia will be allotted under legal enactment for their differing needs in development? Or, as was done for the Indians by the United States of America, will compensation be made to the children for the wrongs done to their fathers?

To both questions unhappily the answer is almost certainly "No."

> No passion so effectually robs the mind of all
> its powers of acting and reasoning as fear.
>
> —Edmund Burke.

As the oncoming white man pushed the aboriginal inhabitants further back from the settled areas, policemen in the more isolated townships were appointed Protectors of Aborigines. In very recent years Aboriginal Welfare Departments came into being with patrol officers to travel the outback country, but the police are still Protectors.

Experience has proved that it is humanly impossible for any man to be an accuser and a protector; the same man cannot prosecute and defend. It is unfair to the police to expect it, and unfair to the aborigines to allow it. Policemen also in some areas are in charge of food rationing for aborigines, and although this presents no temptation to a man of strong character there have been some dismissals because of misappropriation.

Mr F. E. A. Bateman, Royal Commissioner, in a Survey of Native Affairs in Western Australia 1948, reported:

> There are other objectionable features to the system [police as protectors]—equally valid. The aborigines are as a rule in fear of the police and this in itself is an inherent weakness in the system. Moreover in the isolated districts the police officer wields a great deal of power. His word is law and if he happens to be unsympathetic towards the natives then it is a poor

look-out for them. . . . Apart from the fact that many police officers are suitable and efficient protectors it cannot be denied that others are totally unfitted for appointment.

I have met some policemen who were just in their dealings with aborigines, and a few who had real understanding of their difficulties. But the majority had a strong bias against the natives and made no attempt to hide it, as the following cases illustrate.

In May 1935 Billy Joe was brought to Adelaide. He had been a stockman in the Ord River district in Western Australia and had suffered severe injury to his feet as the result of a police patrol. The *Advertiser* 15 May 1935, reported that, with three other aborigines charged with stealing food supplies, he was "foot-walked" a hundred miles in two days over burning stony roads to Wyndham police court. The men were released, but Billy Joe spent months in hospital before he could walk again.

In March 1950 a domestic quarrel in a tribe on the Church of England Edward River Mission, Cape York Peninsula, Queensland, ended in the death of a native policeman. As a reprisal the hunting spears and woomeras of the entire tribe were piled high into a heap and, under the supervision of a Cairns police party, were smashed to pieces. The incident was described by the noted anthropologist Dr Donald Thomson as "a reign of terror." Nearly two weeks later a constable hand-cuffed two aborigines at gunpoint, forced them and two other men with four women and four children to march in front of his horse all night and most of the next day to Coen—a distance of fifty miles—in heavy rain, without food or sleep.

At the subsequent trial of the aborigines the defence sought the help of Dr Thomson and the Crown case collapsed.

On Saturday, 14 May 1955, in Perth Police Court, Constable — said he went to the house of two natives at about 8 p.m. to question them about an alleged offence, following a complaint. The breath of both men smelt of alcohol. He asked the men to go into the street with him for identification. It was found they were not the men concerned. But he arrested both men for being drunk in the street. Both denied the offence, but they were convicted, cautioned, and ordered to pay costs.

Of another case Dr Alfred Jacobs, J.P., of Narrogin, Western Australia, wrote to me:

> In an open Court here on 7 August 1955 a police constable stated in reply to a question from the magistrate that for his own protection he usually carried a revolver when called out to deal with natives. Speaking as a Justice, I am altogether opposed to the use of arms by policemen unless authorized for the particular occasion by an officer of at least the rank of inspector. The constable in this case admitted shooting twice, and the aboriginal concerned was admitted to hospital.

As recently as 1958 at Halls Creek, Western Australia, aboriginal prisoners were reported chained by the ankle to a veranda post while awaiting trial or serving sentence—the eighty-year-old police station had only one cell. A Press report of 20 March 1958 stated:

> A few months ago twelve prisoners were on the chain at the same time. Violent prisoners were described as bodily bound and chained to a ring bolt in the cement floor of the cell. The Deputy Commissioner of Police of Western Australia did not deny the charges, but said in that country the chain method was more humane than handcuffs.

No better illustration of common police attitudes to aborigines could be found than was given by Inspector McKinnon in an interview with the Sydney *Sun* on 11 December 1961. About to retire after thirty years with the Northern Territory police force he said that during the first ten years of his service he had covered 10,000 miles of the inland on camel patrols—"most of it spent chasing native murderers and cattle thieves." He had learnt never to be "weak with natives" and regretted that police were no longer allowed to chain aboriginal prisoners by the neck.

It is hardly necessary to stress the vast difference between police treatment of aborigines and their treatment of the rest of the community.

17

Caste ... Prejudice ... Assimilation

"There's no colour bar in Australia."

"They'll never make the grade."

"They can't hold their liquor."

IT HAS OFTEN been said that half-caste children are despised by both the white and dark races, but that has never been my experience. As children they are treated kindly in our closely settled civilization except by ill-adjusted people; it is true, however, that on the fringe of civilization they are looked at askance. But among tribal full-bloods the odd half-caste child is accepted completely in the family group. The opinion often given that people of mixed blood inherit the worst features of both races has no sound basis and has not been my experience.

It is the half-caste fringe dwellers who have the hardest lot. For them housing, if one can call it that, and hygiene are of the poorest; education is negligible, and after-school training not provided at all. Interest in these people varies with the white man's needs. The men are welcomed during harvest, at shearing time, and for fruit picking, but when seasonal work has finished they have to return to the substandard surroundings that are their homes. In the south-west corner of Western Australia there are many thousands of people of mixed blood living in this way. But shocking conditions exist in some part of every State, and a supreme effort must be made to bring them to an end. Lack of money is the reason usually given by State Governments to explain why enough decent houses and regular work cannot be provided to enable mixed-blood parents to have clean and tidy children acceptable at State public schools.

Other people of mixed blood are living in partly controlled Government settlements or reserves, and only some of these are in full or constant employment; and the state of much of their housing is most unsatisfactory.

In the Northern Territory half-caste children from native camps in the upper North are sent to Melville Island (Roman Catholic), and Croker Island (Methodist), for schooling. In the southern part of the Territory some half-caste children live at the Church of England St Mary's Hostel, Alice Springs, and attend the public school there. Since October 1953 Northern Territory adults of mixed blood have had all the rights of citizenship.

Another group of mixed-bloods are those who have achieved a satisfactory life in the capital cities. Many of these were taken away by mission Sisters from unsatisfactory conditions in the back country in early childhood. They have attended State schools, a local church, learnt a trade or calling and sometimes a profession. Very soon they have become part of the community, and many have done well in adult life. Among the women are double-certificated nurses, teachers including a kindergarten director, and workers in Government welfare departments. Others hold responsible positions in industry and domestic life. Two are matrons of hostels for aboriginal girls.

Men have done equally well; many are in industry, some are engineers, others transport drivers, one a trade union shop steward, one a successful sheep breeder on his own ex-serviceman's property, and four are fully trained teachers. Another man, a gifted singer, is a member of the teaching staff of the Melbourne Conservatorium, while a great responsibility rests on one who is in charge of a Government welfare station. In November 1961 a young man of twenty-three years, after completing a four-year Theology course, was ordained as a Church of Christ minister and was inducted into the charge at Mooroopna in Victoria.

People of mixed blood have been very prominent in various forms of sport. In boxing several have been champions of their weight division, and the late Dave Sands held the Empire middleweight title; many are outstanding in different codes of football, Australian Rules, rugby, and soccer; one has been captain of a first league soccer team and vice-captain for the State; three have been overseas playing in the Rugby League in England. The women too have done well in sport. One played State and International cricket as well as A Grade basketball and hockey, and there are many accomplished players in basketball and hockey throughout the Commonwealth. It is only since the end of the second World War, however, that people of aboriginal descent have been admitted to sports clubs.

Throughout the years there has been too little recognition of our responsibility for the existence of the mixed-blood people —too little concerted effort to provide western amenities of all kinds for the children for whom our race, and our race only, is responsible. The number of people with some aboriginal blood in the settled coastal areas is much greater than is generally realized. Today the greatest increase in their numbers is the result of part-aborigines naturally marrying among themselves.

Full enjoyment of the Australian life and full share in its responsibilities can never be achieved by people of mixed blood unless they feel they are regarded as equals by their fellow Australians. The final test of true social acceptance is the acceptance of the idea of marriage between aborigines and non-aboriginal Australians, although it must be remembered that inter-marriage is not an indispensable condition of assimilation. It is becoming more common in the settled part of the Commonwealth, with the full agreement of the contracting families. The general community, however, through ignorance and prejudice, still regard such marriages with disfavour.

The late Dame Mary Gilmore, whose knowledge of earlier days among aborigines was unrivalled, once told me that in the eighteen-eighties aboriginal men, because they were good artificers, were the blacksmiths in towns and on stations. It was not uncommon for a selector's daughter to become the legal wife of a blacksmith and to be proud of it. When the standards of aborigines in education, hygiene, and home life are similar to ours there can be no valid objection to legal marriages between the two races. Never at any time have they been prohibited by law.

After the ruthlessness of much of the first half of the present century it was hoped the second half would be freer of discrimination against aborigines, but it has proved otherwise.

1951   Fred Waters, a literate, grey-haired aboriginal townsman, for initiating a strike in protest against conditions at Bagot Native Reserve on the outskirts of Darwin, was arrested and banished to Haast Bluff 1,200 miles distant. No charge was ever brought against him.

1952　In December 1952, Des Parfit, a returned soldier in uniform, with Korea war service ribbons on, was refused a meal at a country café because of his being a Westralian aboriginal.

1953　In October 1953 the same man had booked rooms in Perth for his honeymoon. They were cancelled when it was seen that he and his wife were aborigines. With the help of a white lady, other boarding houses were approached, but without success. In great disappointment the young couple had to return home.—*Daily News,* 24 October 1953.

1953　Twenty-two aborigines were arrested on a Sunday, and were charged next day with being in a prohibited area. They had been sitting down in a former tribal ground half a mile from Katherine Township. They were convicted and fined. It was an offence for aborigines to be outside their employer's gate and within one mile of the township after dark and on holidays.—*The News,* Adelaide, 28 April 1953.

1955　Early in this year a mission for half-caste children at Oodnadatta in South Australia applied for admission of its children to the local public school. Following vigorous protests from a number of white people an inspector was sent to investigate. The application was refused, but the following year the State Education Department ruled that aboriginal children if clean and tidy could attend school. This allowed mission children to attend but excluded "camp" children who, without housing, cannot meet the requirements. Houses have not yet been built.—*The Mail,* Adelaide, 17 March 1956.

1955　At Moree, New South Wales, aborigines and part-aborigines were banned from swimming in the town pool and from using municipal buildings.—*The Advertiser,* 13 June 1955.

1956　At York in Western Australia an immigrant café proprietor refused two well-dressed aborigines a cup of coffee, stating that mixing black and white was bad for business. —*Westralian Aborigine.*

1957   A hotel-keeper in Pinjarra, West Australia, refused to admit an aboriginal Methodist Mission Sister who was booked in with the Superintendent and his wife. The Superintendent, a Methodist Minister, refused to compromise with accommodation at the back of the hotel for the Sister, and the party left.—*The Age,* Melbourne, 31 August 1957.

1958   The Town Council of Kempsey, New South Wales, placed a colour bar on its swimming pool although the aborigines were members of the Surf Club. Wauchope, a near-by town, invited the men to use its pool and to swim at its carnival.—*The News,* Adelaide, 21 January 1958.

1958   Several residents of Drouin, forty-six miles from Melbourne, protested against a quarter-caste family taking a house in the town.—*The Advertiser,* 24 September 1958.

1958   A picture theatre owner at Pialba, 188 miles north of Brisbane, admitted that she segregated aboriginal patrons from whites.—*The News,* 14 October 1958.

1958   Twenty-six white people signed a petition to Nambucca Shire Council, New South Wales, protesting against the sale of a house to an aboriginal family although they enjoyed full citizenship rights. The family mixed freely with the townsfolk; the man was in regular employment and paid income tax. He was also a stalwart in rugby league football. This action created public resentment and, when the house in question was sold to a local baker, the aboriginal family was encouraged and helped with the purchase of a near-by block for building on.—*The Advertiser,* 23 August 1958.

1959   A charming full-blood girl of eleven years, an ex-patient of the Children's Hospital, Adelaide, and a frequent guest in our home, was to return north with a white mother and her three young children. At a railway junction ticket office the mother was refused a booking in a Commonwealth Railway second class sleeper for the aboriginal girl. The mother phoned me. I reported the matter to railway headquarters and sleepers for all were provided—but only after a week's delay.—Personal record.

1961   In January 1961 aborigines at Woodenbong, New South Wales, accused white citizens of wholesale discrimination against them. A much-respected aboriginal man who ran a modern hire-car was interviewed and stated that his people were looked at askance in cafés and picture theatres, where they had to sit apart. "The local policeman started a wonderful youth club. It was to have had both coloured and white children and it did to start with. But then the whites decided to take their children out of the club unless our coloured youngsters left it; so our children had to go."—*The Advertiser,* 4 January 1961.

1961   In August 1961 two aboriginal trainee teachers and two New Guinea natives, one of them a member of the Legislative Council, were refused accommodation at a Brisbane Hotel. "We never take dark people," was the hotel-keeper's reply. Arriving in Brisbane to work on exhibits from New Guinea and the Northern Territory at the Brisbane National Show, they were welcomed at the airport by Mr L. van der Heyden, a Territories Department official, who described the action of the hotel as "shocking."—*The Advertiser,* 9 August 1961.

1961   In September it happened again in Queensland—"No coloured person will ever be served in our hotel," said the manager of a hotel in Townsville. When told he had refused a Kenya education officer on an exchange Commonwealth instructional tour of Australia he replied: "I did not stop to inquire who he was. He was black —and that was enough." An apology followed the Prime Minister's intervention on behalf of the Commonwealth guest. But investigation showed that forty-one out of forty-two hotels in Townsville refuse to serve coloured people.—*The Advertiser,* 20 September 1961.

1962   At Elliot township in the Northern Territory when five aboriginal children went to school at the beginning of the year, the seven white children were withdrawn by their parents.

The foregoing incidents, all in the last decade, make it manifest that until there is radical alteration in the attitude of white people to our aborigines the question of assimilation is an impossibility.

In the transition to our way of life much will depend on the aborigines themselves, but the greater responsibility is ours, for we have forced the change upon them. When their tribal land was taken from them to fatten sheep and cattle, independent living by hunting and gathering became impossible. To remain alive the aborigines had to adopt a dependent life, accepting what food was offering at station homesteads in return for which their work was demanded.

In tribal life energy was expended in the struggle to keep alive, but in the more settled life of sheep and cattle stations, in exchange for even meagre food, the station owners expected the aborigines to devote their whole energy to work on the stations. It did not occur to employers that routine and long hours of work, without apparent reason, were concepts utterly incomprehensible to tribal aborigines. After a time inadequate diet sapped the strength of the aboriginal workers; this, coupled with the disturbance of mind resulting from the subversion of their age-long philosophy and religion, caused the aborigines to falter in a state of bewilderment.

It was not generally recognized either that tribal life in all its aspects was intimately linked with religious beliefs and rites: now by comparison they were entering a world largely devoid of religion. The aborigines, following on faithful performance of tribal rites, trusted implicitly in the Sky Hero to supply their needs; but the white man, they found, had little faith in anything but himself and worried about everything. Not less confused were they by our competitive way of life with its greed, selfishness, and amassing of wealth—so alien to their communal living and sharing with others. It was not to be expected that men interested only in profits would understand or attempt to understand the dilemma of the aborigines.

In our approach to the full-bloods we must remember that the family is the basis of their lives as it is of ours. Young children should never be separated from their parents and housed in dormitories or institutions. If for urgent medical reasons a child must be taken to hospital it must go with the consent of its parents, who must be kept advised of its progress. Attempts at assimilation by bringing very bright individual aborigines into the white community is cruel and wrong. As Gordon Sweeney, a patrol officer of long and valued service in Northern Territory Welfare, said: "It is overlooked that the only safe assimilation is that based on stable family and social life." And it certainly should not be demanded that those entering our way of life should give up all contact with their full-blood relatives.

Assimilation of the part-aborigines, the great majority of whom have been compulsorily educated in State schools, should be a much simpler process, but unfortunately full social acceptance has sometimes been denied those who have risen to positions of trust. Successful assimilation depends above all on an enlightened attitude on race, and the complete elimination of colour prejudice.

In support of the claim that assimilation need not mean complete absorption of the native race it is interesting to note what has happened in the United States of America and in New Zealand as the result of new and enlightened policies. In the United States not only has there been a substantial increase in the Indian population; there has also been some maintenance of separate cultural groups. In New Zealand the increase in people of Maori blood was from 42,000 in 1896 to 158,300 in 1960, and in New Zealand too there is considerable evidence that Maori culture in certain parts of the country is likely to continue.

In Australia the number of people known to have aboriginal blood—full or part—is at least one hundred thousand, apart from the many merged in the white population. Aboriginal people are proud of their heritage, just as Scots or Irish, English or Welsh are of their ancestry, and the full-blood increase that has taken place since 1939 could lead to a recovery of the dignity and independence that was theirs in earlier days.

Preservation of cultural grouping, where it is still possible, and pride in aboriginal heritage should be encouraged. It is something of which we could be proud in days to come.

If the policy of assimilation is to succeed, the purely paternal control of the past must cease, and a new approach be made through specially trained personnel who can appreciate the feelings of the aborigines in their time of transfer from their way of life to ours. The aim must always be to enable the aborigines to retain the self-respect and independence they had in tribal days.

Assimilation is not absorption. At the first conference on Aboriginal Welfare of Commonwealth and State authorities in 1937 the then Commissioner of Native Affairs in Western Australia advocated absorption to the extent that we would "eventually forget that there ever were any aborigines in Australia." Such a state of affairs was never, in my opinion, in the mind of the Minister for Territories, the Hon Paul Hasluck when he introduced the present policy of assimilation. It meant, he said, "that to survive and prosper the aborigines must live and work and think as white Australians do, so that they can take their place in social, economic, and political equality with the rest of the Australian community."

In the cities of Australia some mingling of the dark and white people has already taken place, with part-aborigines living and working in the white community, but it will be many years before a similar condition, based on respect, exists in the back country. There must be a great change in outlook on the part of the white community of Australia, for there are many places in the inland and in the north where human rights are completely ignored. Tribal aborigines are people of dignity with pride of race, and since 1939 full-bloods have increased in number, in some places markedly.

We have no right to force them to change, but as we have usurped their land and made their old life almost impossible it is incumbent on us to provide the means by which they can change to our ways if they wish. There is no future for them unless we meet them with full respect, recognizing their worth as human beings, and providing training in health and the hygiene of settled life. They must receive education as we know it, and be trained in trades and callings with a view to employment.

While in Darwin in 1951 I made an investigation into the question of aborigines and the consumption of alcohol. I found that it was an offence by ordinance for an aboriginal to drink alcohol, and it was an offence by ordinance for a white person to employ an aboriginal in licensed premises. Yet I was told that the definition of "licensed premises" was so vague that it would be almost impossible to secure a conviction. It was further explained to me that it was an offence for a native to be on licensed premises, but was not an offence in law for a licensee to allow the native on his licensed premises if he, the hotelkeeper, had a licence to employ aborigines. Under Northern Territory law it seemed that the only step that could be taken against the employment of aborigines in hotels was to refuse hotelkeepers a licence to employ natives in any way.

On Thursday, 12 July 1951, ten aborigines—six men and four women—from Adelaide River township were charged in the Darwin Police Court with—

(a) drinking alcohol
(b) receiving liquor
(c) stealing liquor
(d) breaking and entering premises for liquor.

For (a) each aboriginal was fined two pounds, with ten shillings costs. Nine of the ten were first offenders.

For (b) each aboriginal was given twenty-eight days' hard labour. For (c) and (d) each was committed for trial before the Supreme Court.

It was admitted in Court that several of the ten were employed in the hotel taking used bottles from the bar to the back premises. The little alcohol that was in each used bottle was poured into a container and the supply then shared. An aboriginal gave this information when being examined. The hotel licensee was not charged, presumably because of the legal tangle already mentioned. The fine for an aboriginal found drinking alcohol was two pounds, with ten shillings costs—more than a week's wages.

In Court I saw white men who had been arrested while incapably drunk, and not for a first offence, fined five shillings with seven shillings and sixpence costs, a mere fraction of a day's wage.

On making inquiries I was told frankly that very few members of the white population who had the handling of natives were abstainers from alcoholic beverages. At a Court of Appeal for an increased wage in Darwin while I was there, it was stated that most men in Darwin spent between two pounds and three pounds a week on alcohol. With the legal provision of alcoholic liquor for the white man, how can the aboriginal be expected to regard the drinking of alcohol as an offence? The aborigines in

Darwin can never get away from alcohol; they see it on every hand by day, and at night illicit white traders bring it by taxi to their compounds. According to Magistrate J. Crang, quoted in the *Northern Standard,* of 23 March 1951, the traffic was at that time wide open.

It is commonly believed that aborigines are more susceptible to the effects of alcohol than the white man, but there is no physiological proof at all of this. Social and economic discrimination against the aboriginal, and the frustration and bitterness resulting therefrom almost certainly explain the fact that so many aborigines turn to drink. Knowing it is an offence by law, they drink quickly to avoid detection and in this way increase the toxic effects of the drug. It is blatant discrimination that it is lawful for a man with a white skin to drink alcohol freely, but that it is illegal for an aboriginal with a dark skin to touch it.

T. G. H. Strehlow, Reader in Linguistics at Adelaide University, and a man with life-long contact with aborigines, stated publicly in January 1960 that "for most aborigines liquor had become the symbol of emancipation, of equality with the white man, and of full Australian citizenship." For that tragic estimate of our citizenship the white man is responsible.

What force of argument have we to convince the aborigines of the grave danger of alcohol to mind and body when they see white people freely imbibing it every day in the townships, and taking it as a beverage on cattle stations, settlements, and even on some missions? Is it any wonder the native regards the drinking of alcohol as a special privilege he longs to share? They are not to know that we have now three hundred thousand alcoholics in Australia's population.

It is serious enough for part-aborigines in our towns to witness the trade in alcohol, but far worse is the danger to tribal aborigines when at two cattle stations in the southern part of the Northern Territory a licence has been given to sell liquor. It is, however, not from licensed premises that the worst form of intoxicant is supplied.

In 1937 there were persistent rumours of white men trafficking in methylated spirits among aborigines in the country served by the Birdum-Darwin railway. The allegations were investigated by the Chief Protector of Aborigines in the Northern Territory and by the police. Their report to the Administrator stated that at one place along the railway line methylated spirits was sold at two shillings a bottle over the counter and two shillings and threepence off a wet-bag—the substitute for ice. In January 1938 about forty gallons were said to have been sent down the line and that this was the monthly average for 1937.

In Darwin in September 1939 allegations were made by two responsible settlers from the interior that many Northern Territory buffalo shooters, peanut growers, and some station owners were supplying methylated spirits to aborigines in their employment in place of proper payment in kind. The Director of Native Affairs, Mr E. W. P. Chinnery, said he believed the alleged trafficking existed, but to ensure a successful prosecution the offender would have to be caught red-handed and "a tremendous staff would be needed."

In 1959 I wrote to the Director of Native Welfare in the Northern Territory, Mr H. C. Giese, for the latest information on the matter. He replied that there were still some problems in relation to the supply of liquor and methylated spirits to aborigines in and around Darwin, but the practice did not extend south of Darwin along the railway. Eradication, he said, would continue to be difficult while unscrupulous white persons were prepared to supply spirits to the natives for gain.

That alcohol is bedevilling the citizenship of aborigines is undeniable. Full citizenship rights for them are being opposed by many white people solely because they fear that aborigines with legal access to alcohol will drink to excess. From personal knowledge I can say that aborigines who want alcohol have no great difficulty in getting it by stealth; but their white suppliers take care to provide them with only the cheapest stuff at exorbitant prices.

It may be that for two years or so after restrictions are removed, drinking among aborigines will increase, but in my opinion drunkenness among them will soon be much less than it is today. Aborigines in Victoria moved into full citizenship in 1957, and since then no increase in drinking has been reported. Few will deny that aboriginal people living in our community should have the same legal rights as we have. Denial of rights on the score of colour or race is incompatible with basic human justice and should cease.

There is urgent need for education of aborigines on the danger of alcohol as a beverage. Pastor Albrecht has issued a pamphlet in the Aranda language for the darker citizens of Alice Springs where drinking is rife even among teenagers. This is a step in the right direction, and should be followed up on missions and settlements.

In the interest of both races there is a strong case for simple scientific education about alcohol and its effects on the human body, whether white or dark.

18

A Man's a Man For a' That

EVEN AT THIS LATE date there are many people in Australia who can see nothing good in our aborigines. Personally I have found more trust, love, sharing, and sacrifice among tribal and semi-tribal aborigines than in many white people.

Early in this century Inspector Johns, of Adelaide, owed his life to just such qualities in a tribal full-blood, when he was a constable in the police force of the Northern Territory. He was taking Neighbour to Leichhardt police station on a charge of cattle spearing. In crossing a raging torrent half a mile wide the policeman swam on one side of the horse and the prisoner on the other. In mid-stream the horse became terrified, and kicked the policeman, rendering him almost unconscious. Neighbour reached the bank, but seeing the policeman's plight he wound the chain round his body and plunged in. In spite of the hazard of crocodiles he swam to Johns, brought him to land, and looked after him until he recovered.

For this act of courage Neighbour was awarded the Royal Albert Medal. Years later, when I was attending the Inspector, during an illness, he still spoke feelingly of the incident. A revealing comment on the story of Neighbour was made by a sergeant of police who walked into the Australian Board of Missions headquarters in Sydney. He complained that the white people outback did not approve of the Church taking the part of the blacks, and that too much was being made of the incident. "It is nothing very wonderful," he said, "for the blackfellows always act like that."

In the same decade there occurred in the Northern Territory a moving illustration of the ennobling influence an untutored aboriginal woman had upon a white man. The man told me his story in 1951 as he lay ill in Katherine Hospital, twenty-three years after the woman's death. He had met her as a young tribal woman, and at their first meeting there was a strong mutual attraction. After a time she consented to live with him. He taught her simple English, and such religion as he had learned. Presently she pleaded with him to stop drinking and swearing. For a time he did so, but one Saturday he came home madly drunk, swearing, and violent.

Next day, when he had come to his senses, Maggie spoke seriously to her husband—for that is what he was—about the things he had taught her. She made him realize the damage he had done to his wife and to his home, and he was so overcome that he never to the day of his death touched alcohol again. When Maggie died there was no place for her in the white man's cemetery. Her husband sewed her body in hessian, carried it across the river and buried her in the sand. Soon afterwards he erected a metal fence round the grave, planted flowers and kept them watered. A brass plate was put up and on it "Maggie 13.2.28." In one of his letters to me he wrote: "If Maggie is not in heaven I don't want to go there."

Nor is the often-despised, naked nomad lacking in the same warm human qualities. In 1933 a white man, attempting to cross a mountain range on horseback, lay helpless on the ground with a fractured pelvis. Had not a tribal man and his wife chanced that way he would have died. The woman stayed by the injured man while her husband climbed over two steep ranges to the nearest settlement for help. When the rescue party arrived the two primitive aborigines picked up digging-stick and piti, hunting spears and woomera, and went on their way.

A story of great devotion shown by a medicine man to a fellow-tribesman comes from Caledon Bay. In May 1937 an aboriginal there realized he had contracted leprosy. Kangoola, the medicine man, wanted to treat him, but the sick man had once been at Roper police station and asked to be taken there for the white man's medicine. Kangoola carried the man on his back for three hundred miles, and in the process had to swim flooded, quickly flowing rivers, wade through extensive swamps, and risk crocodiles in the many rivers crossed.

Often they were halted by torrential rains, and nine months passed before they reached the police station. While they were travelling in their own country Kangoola was helped by members of their tribe, but even in strange country, natives, at other times hostile, cared for the sick man and his carrier. At the end of the long journey Kangoola must have found his reward hard to understand—he was held in the island leprosarium in Darwin Harbour as a contact.

Not long after this came another example of courage and fellowship in Arnhem Land. A canoe crossing the mouth of the Liverpool River was capsized by a shark, and the aborigines were thrown into the river. Being powerful swimmers they reached the shore in safety, but one of them, returning for the canoe, was attacked by the shark. As soon as he yelled, his companions dived to his rescue and drove off the shark by splashing. The man had lost a leg, but was brought ashore and tended by his fellow tribesmen. He survived the immediate shock and eventually made a good recovery.

Late in April 1939 it was reported in the Press that "grave concern" was felt for the safety of a Darwin pilot lost in Arnhem Land where the aborigines "were reputed to be the most dangerous in Australia." But after a few days' intensive air search he was found beside a native camp. The tribal aborigines had given him water and food, and built him a shelter. Not only that, but braving the high seas caused by recent storms two of the nomads paddled in a dug-out canoe to Goulburn Island from where radio contact was made with Darwin.

Another white man was succoured in his distress early in January 1940. Fred Hardy, owner of a cattle station near the head of the Alligator River in Arnhem Land, was the only white man on the station. In a motor accident he had broken his leg; his aboriginal stockmen came to his rescue and drove him in a motor truck fifty miles over country that had been turned into deep mud by torrential rain. Eventually they reached the Mary River, which was in flood. One of the natives swam the river, and then ran ten miles to Pine Creek township for help, while the others made a raft and ferried Hardy across the roaring torrent. A truck then took the injured man to Pine Creek, where he was picked up by a light plane from Darwin and flown to hospital there.

During the same cyclonic storm the Roper River in south Arnhem Land was fifteen miles wide, and, whipped up by terrific wind, did great damage. At the Roper River Mission everything was lost. Flood waters were twenty feet over the mission house, and the lugger of ten tons with the mission staff on board was smashed by a huge tree. The aboriginal crew, disregarding all danger to themselves, swam with the missionaries to near-by tree-tops where they clung throughout the night with the waters swirling all around them. Next day the aborigines transferred the staff to high ground before going for help. It took them three days to reach Roper River police station where they found the constable marooned with natives he had saved. After a brief rest they pressed on to Roper Valley station, another two days' trip by foot, and by dug-out canoe round the outskirts of the flood. "It was amazing that the natives reached here at all," said the owner of the station.

In October 1952 Samuel Pootchemunka of the Aurukun Mission was on a fishing trip, and was paddling his dug-out canoe up the Archer River. With him were his daughter-in-law and her ten-month-old baby. Without warning a crocodile reared behind the canoe and pulled the woman into the water. Like a flash the man leapt at the brute, grabbed it in his arms and sank his fingers fiercely into its eyes. The crocodile loosened its hold, and the man carried the young woman to the bank. Immediately he returned to the river for the infant who was nowhere to be seen in the muddy water. Then something touched his back—the baby had floated to the surface. He swam to the bank, where he revived the baby, and then gave his attention to the mother who was badly shocked and severely torn by the crocodile's claws. The tide was against them, so they had to wait until it turned, and eight hours passed before they reached Aurukun Mission. The woman was taken to the Cairns Hospital, where she recovered. Pootchemunka was awarded the Royal Humane Society's Silver Medal for bravery.

Aurukun Mission of the Presbyterian Church is proud of the fact that another of its natives was awarded a silver medal two years later. This time Porelembin Woolla nearly lost his life in trying to save his employer. The two men were together in a boat owned by the white man when it sank about two hundred yards from the shore in a shark-infested and stormy sea. The tide was racing, but the native was a powerful swimmer and he tried to haul his companion, who could not swim, to the shore. When the white man lost consciousness the aboriginal encircled his body with his right arm, and with immense effort struggled on. But he was tiring; several times he lost his grip, but each time dived and brought the man to the surface again. It was by then a desperate struggle of will. Forty minutes later the two men were pulled aboard a launch. Joyce, the white man, still held like a vice in the aboriginal's rigid arm, was dead, but Woolla, completely exhausted and unconscious, was resuscitated in hospital.

These stories culled over the years are told simply to show that courage and selflessness are found in the human heart the world over. But the existence of these qualities in the aborigines of Australia has generally been ignored and often emphatically denied.

Epilogue

EVERY AUSTRALIAN HAS the right to expect the satisfaction of his basic human needs—food, shelter, work, and acceptance. But not yet have all these been accorded our aborigines, and the most serious lack is the first of them—food.

Indigenous people, wherever they are, when forced to give up their traditional way of life and to adopt a very different social economy, have suffered from malnutrition. In aboriginal tribal life a varied diet, with meat as the chief item, was the rule, but contact with our civilization changed the fare to flour, tea, and sugar, with little meat and sometimes none at all. This resulted in a serious lack of protein, with undermining of the health of the now semi-tribal people, the men becoming unequal to prolonged hard work, and the women unfit to bear sturdy children.

Infant mortality among Australian aborigines in these circumstances has been appallingly high—"two hundred deaths in the first year of life to every one thousand born"—and malnutrition has been the chief cause of death, not diarrhoea or pneumonia, to which they may eventually have succumbed.

That a baby was fat before it was taken ill does not necessarily mean that the child was properly fed, for examination of the distended abdomen often reveals an enlarged liver, the result of chronic malnutrition. The wastage of aboriginal babies and toddlers over the years of our occupation of Australia must cease. Trained women welfare workers must be appointed to instruct aboriginal mothers in nutrition and hygiene, and correct food must be supplied to all mothers and babies. Kwashiorkor, that dread disease of the undernourished child on the edge of civilization, must not be allowed to become established in Australia.

Unemployment of aboriginal full-blood men is another matter that needs serious and immediate attention. There has never been a plan for full employment of our aborigines whose hunting days are over. In recent years even the work they could expect to find in the interior is rapidly decreasing as a result of mechanization—the old boundary-rider and the cattle-droving team are rapidly becoming a vivid memory of Australia's past. Yet the number of full-bloods is increasing year by year. The dilemma —man-power without work—must be faced.

For people of aboriginal blood who have entered our civilization, the great majority of whom are part white, the first essential is housing. Without a home they cannot take their place among us with dignity, yet proper housing has been provided for only very few.

Finally, it is my conviction that the time is due when the Federal Government must be allowed to assume responsibility for aborigines in all States as well as for those in the Northern Territory. In the past our treatment of these people has been a national shame. Their happier future is a national responsibility. But no amount of legislative progress will compensate for the saddest obstacle to that happier future—the refusal of a majority of white Australians to recognize the worth of the aborigines and to accept them.

The responsibility for this refusal lies heavily with members of the Christian Church. It is we who profess to apply the spirit and teaching of Christ to the solution of all human problems. If in 1788 and throughout the following years the Christian Church had directed its mind to the dilemma of the aborigines, if it had maintained an uncompromising stand on their just treatment, then this fine race would long since have become a proud and happy part of the Australian nation.